MAPS

British North America..4

British Possessions in the West Indies........................5

Burgoyne's Campaign and the Battle of Saratoga............7

British North America as a Possibility.....................9

The Siege of Charleston..11

British Outposts in South Carolina and Georgia............13

Backcountry Militia Actions..................................15

Battle of Camden 17

Marion's Engagements August 1780-September 1781.....19

Movements Leading to King's Mountain...............22-23

Battle of King's Mountain..24

Greene Divides his Army..32

Troop Movements Leading to Cowpens............... 34-35

Battle of Cowpens: Initial Deployment………………… 37

Battle of Cowpens: Tarleton's Advance…………………38

Battle of Cowpens: Flanking Move Attempted…………..39

Battle of Cowpens: Patriot Counter-Attack……………..40

Race to the Dan……………………………………….42-43

Battle at Guilford Courthouse……………………....…46

Troop Movements After Guilford Courthouse……..……48

British North America After Guilford Courthouse..……..52

Camden, Fort Watson and Fort Motte……………...……54

Battle of Hobkirk's Hill……………………………....…..56

Augusta and Ninety-Six……………………………...…...59

Siege of Ninety-Six………………………………...……..62

Marion's Route to Parker's Ferry…………..……………72

Greene's Route from High Hills to Burdell's...…………..75

Battle of Eutaw Springs…………………………..104-105

British Retreat to Ferguson's Swamp………………….121

Yorktown……………………………………………….127

British North America After Yorktown…………………133

FOREWORD

The Valiant Died is Christine Swager's fourth book and she clearly is on a mission. Her mission is the same as all teachers and historians: to push back the frontiers of ignorance and indifference that obscures the South's Revolutionary War heritage. The book you hold in your hand is her latest thrust against that frontier, and I think you will agree that we have gained ground. In this intriguing survey of the southern campaign that ends in a bloody set-piece battle at Eutaw Springs, Swager reveals the strategy, tactics, and heroism that won America her independence.

Christine will tell you she is not an historian but a "storyteller." Yet, she is a storyteller who takes great and exacting pains to "get it right." To get it right means that she must do what historians do; search diligently and thoroughly for sources that reveal the past, analyze them carefully, and put them in an engaging narrative. So, don't be fooled. This "story" is as much history as any historian would write.

Perhaps what Christine means by being a storyteller rather than an historian is that her target audience is not the professional historian. She writes for a different audience. She holds knowledge's right flank for young Americans who will someday pass on our heritage to another generation. She knows that if this generation does not know its past, and cherish it, ignorance and indifference will destroy them just a surely as a Brown Bess musket ball at thirty yards. The goal is to write history that excites people to know more about the War for Independence; to go searching in archives and libraries to find out for themselves what happened between 1775 and 1783.

The story of Eutaw Springs is especially needed and timely. Here is one battlefield that indifference has just about destroyed. Today, the only reminder of that sanguinary event is a small park in the little hamlet near Eutawville, South Carolina. It is surrounded by urbanization and water. An unknown portion of the battlefield is either under Lake Marion, or disturbed by industry and houses. I say an unknown portion because presently we just do not know how much of the battlefield might still exist, if not as landscape, maybe as an archaeological resource. What is needed is a combined landscape, historical, and archaeological study that would determine how much is left of this critical battlefield. With such a study, a plan could be made to salvage what is endangered and preserve what can still be protected for future generations. With better knowledge of the battlefield, an interpretive program could be developed for tourists and students. A program of preservation and battlefield interpretation would be a great achievement. It is the duty of the present generation to hold fast to the past, and to pass it on to the future. The Eutaw Springs battlefield is a sacred place- a shared heritage and it must be preserved.

As readers of *The Valiant Died* will soon learn, the Battle of Eutaw Springs was the last great battle in the south during the American Revolution. With the bludgeoning at Eutaw Springs, the British were forced to retreat to Charleston and America's victory in the south was all but complete, awaiting only the surrender at Yorktown. The fighting was fierce and heroism was the norm on both sides. Nathanael Greene was at his best, with his top commanders at his front: Francis Marion, Andrew Pickens, Henry Lee, William Washington, Otho Williams, John Eager Howard, Jethro Sumner, Wade Hampton, Robert Kirkwood, Richard Campbell. These are names that all Americans should know.

The British too were, well British – cool, aggressive, disciplined and deadly. Eutaw Springs demonstrated that the Americans, Continentals and militia, would stand and trade volley for volley with the world's finest professional soldiers. Who won? It does not matter. What does matter is that the Americans thought they had won, and that's often all that counts in war. What matters today is that Eutaw Springs was a battle we must not forget, and Christine Swager keeps it in our memory in *The Valiant Died.*

Enjoy and remember.

Steven D. Smith, Archaeologist
South Carolina Institute of Archaeology and Anthropology

THE VALIANT DIED

The Battle of Eutaw Springs
September 8, 1781

Christine R. Swager
Maps by John Robertson

HERITAGE BOOKS
2007

HERITAGE BOOKS
AN IMPRINT OF HERITAGE BOOKS, INC.

Books, CDs, and more—Worldwide

For our listing of thousands of titles see our website at
www.HeritageBooks.com

Published 2007 by
HERITAGE BOOKS, INC.
Publishing Division
65 East Main Street
Westminster, Maryland 21157-5026

Copyright © 2006 Christine R. Swager
Maps Copyright © 2006 John Robertson

All rights reserved. No part of this book may be reproduced or transmitted in any form or by any means, electronic or mechanical, including photocopying, recording or by any information storage and retrieval system without written permission from the author, except for the inclusion of brief quotations in a review.

International Standard Book Number: 978-0-7884-4102-8

Eutaw Springs

At Eutaw Springs the valiant died
Their limbs with dust are covered o'er:
Weep on, ye springs, your tearful tide:
How many heroes are no more!

By Philip Freneau

CONTENTS

LIST OF MAPS……………………………………. ……..vii

FOREWORD by Steven Smith…………………………....ix

ACKNOWLEDGMENTS………………………………..xiii

INTRODUCTION…………………………………………xv

CHAPTER I: The War Comes to the South ……….....……1

CHAPTER II: Trouble in the Back Country……………....25

CHAPTER III: Greene's Decision………………………..49

CHAPTER IV: At the High Hills……………………….65

CHAPTER V: Greene's American Army…………………79

CHAPTER VI: The British Army……………………….91

CHAPTER VII: The Battle……………………………101

CHAPTER VIII: The Aftermath……………………….115

CHAPTER IX: Yorktown…………………………….. ...125

CHAPTER X: Who Won the Battle of Eutaw Springs?..135

APPENDIX……………………………………………...145

ENDNOTES………………………………………..….161

BIBLIOGRAPHY……………………………………….165

INDEX……………………………………………….…..169

ABOUT THE AUTHORS………………………………175

ACKNOWLEDGMENTS

To be a storyteller among serious scholars and avid historians could be intimidating. However, that community has been most gracious with their support and encouragement. From the beginning Dr. Walter Edgar, George Washington Professor of History at The University of South Carolina, has been a constant source of support. He has sponsored my work in many venues, read manuscripts, included me in programs and recommended my stories to teachers, as well as a wider congregation of readers. His efforts have opened many doors for me and I am grateful.

John Buchanan, author of ***The Road to Guilford Courthouse*** and ***The Road to Valley Forge****,* is another scholar who has given his time and his advice to help me tell the stories. He interrupted his own research to read this manuscript. In a careful examination he found errors and points which needed to be clarified.

Charles Baxley, editor of the ***Southern Campaigns of the American Revolution***, also read a late manuscript and made suggestions.

Stephen Smith has supported my efforts through this and three previous books. He read the first draft of a story about Eutaw Springs when I was still hesitant about the venture. He encouraged me to continue, made suggestions about an approach, directed me to sources and read subsequent manuscripts.

Dr. Lawrence Babits graciously allowed me to base my story of Cowpens on his research. Dr. Bobby Moss has fielded many questions. Patrick O'Kelley, whose work encompasses a colossal amount of Revolutionary War research, is always prompt in responding to my inquiries.

Friends Sheila and Arlie Church, avocational historians and re-enactors, read an early draft. Their suggestions led me to sources documenting the role of North Carolinians in the battle of Eutaw Springs.

A chance meeting and conversation at Cowpens with Calvin and LaVerne Myers produced a copy of the handwritten pension application of an ancestor who served with the North Carolina militia and accompanied British prisoners back to Salisbury, North Carolina.

I have benefitted from the expertise and assistance of those who cherish this history. If errors persist, they are mine.

To understand the 'how' and 'why' of Eutaw Springs requires a review of the events which lead Nathanael Greene to this battle site. Believing it is important that the reader be aware of the geography of the area and the terrain of the sites, I turned again to John Robertson. John assembled and/or constructed maps to accompany every phase of the narrative so that the reader can follow the story of what happened. I appreciate his dedication to this effort.

The use of period maps engendered some difficulty with spelling consistency. In the early days locations were identified by who owned them: Musgrove's Mill, King's Mountain and Hobkirk's Hill. Present usage has dropped the possessives. Other changes have been made over the years, such as Quinby for Quimby. I have retained the old spellings where possible.

The final contributions to this effort were made by Corinne Will and Roxanne Carlson of Heritage Books. Their support and expertise are greatly appreciated.

In this long and sometimes frustrating process, my husband, Bob, has been a tower of strength. None of this would have been possible without his constant encouragement.

Christine R. Swager

INTRODUCTION

On January 10, 1822, William Johnson wrote:

> The bloody fields of the Eutaws, Cowpens and Guilford, remain undistinguished by any expression of Public Reminiscence. The two former are dasert (sic) wilds. But they are classic ground, and should the public patronage follow this effort of my pen, the traveler shall no longer pass these hallowed spots, unheeding, that he treads upon the mould that has been moistened by the best blood of our country. (Johnson, 1822:x).

Today, over two hundred years later, the sites of the Battle of Cowpens and the Battle of Guilford Courthouse are protected and preserved by the National Park Service. What of the Eutaws, the site of the bloodiest battle of the Revolutionary War, the Battle of Eutaw Springs?

On the morning of 6 September 1781, the American Forces, commanded by Major General Nathanael Greene, met a British force, commanded by Lieutenant Colonel Alexander Stewart, on this field. The battle, which lasted about four hours in the suffocating South Carolina heat, is described as the bloodiest battle of the Revolution. When the battle ended over three hundred men lay dead on the field, and seven hundred soldiers were wounded, many mortally so. Participants reported wading through puddles of blood! Many of the dead were buried where they fell.

On the shore of Lake Marion in Orangeburg County, South Carolina, about two acres of occasionally mowed field commemorate the place. Water from a man-made lake floods the springs which supplied early Indian encampments with pure water. Later, settlers camped there during their travels and campaigns. The creek which flowed from the springs to the Santee River is now flooded and boats dot the shore. Houses cover the area where the battle was fought. The unmarked graves are beyond the road, under houses, in cultivated fields, along the docks. Few know that they tread on sacred ground, the burial place of over three hundred who were interred beneath that sod.

The small park set aside to commemorate this battle is marked with a metal plaque with the date of the battle, 8 September 1781. Little else. To add to the casual visitor's bewilderment is a single grave with an engraved capstone marking the resting place of Major John Marjoribanks, a British officer who heroically commanded a flank infantry battalion at the battle. Mortally wounded in the last stages of the battle, he died and was buried at a plantation nearby. When Santee-Cooper flooded his resting place, he was moved here.

There is nothing on the site which would inform the visitor that history was made here. The traveler still passes "this hallowed spot, unheeding, that he treads upon the mould that has been moistened by the best blood of our country."

The purpose of this book is to give the reader some perspective on the battle and information about the participants and events. It is hoped that, in the future, funding will enable military historians to examine the battlefield and to write an in-depth account of the Battle of Eutaw Springs.

Christine R. Swager
Santee, South Carolina
September 2005

CHAPTER I

THE WAR MOVES TO THE SOUTH

In the early days of September 1781 Major General Nathanael Greene led his ragtag army along the road on the south side of the Santee River in South Carolina. The American army, battle weary, ill-clothed, ill-equipped, pursued a force of well-trained and well-armed British troops. The British forces were encamped at Eutaw Springs, named for the two springs which provided fresh water from the underground caverns. It was the most pleasant site for a camp that could be found in the heat and humidity of the late summer.

On 8 September 1781 the American army attacked the British force and the Battle of Eutaw Springs changed the expectations of the British. A month before the surrender of the British Army under the command of Lord Cornwallis at Yorktown, the American commander, Major General Nathanael Greene, had taken back all the territory that the British had occupied in Cornwallis' campaign through the south. The only exceptions were the ports of Charleston and Savannah.

This is the story of how the strategy of Nathanael Greene and the sacrifices and suffering of his troops were able to reclaim territory which England had hoped to maintain regardless of the final outcome of the war.

Consider the audacity of the settlers of the thirteen colonies who challenged the power of the British Empire. After defeating France in the Seven Years' War (called the French and Indian War in North America), Great Britain was the most powerful nation on earth. Aptly, "the sun never set on the British Empire." In this hemisphere most of the settled territory on the Atlantic belonged to Great Britain. Further, the British Navy ruled the seas. The British Army was considered the finest in the world. Yet thirteen of the American colonies challenged the might of the British Empire because, as British subjects, they objected to the policies of the English Parliament (Cook, 1995).

Although there had been demonstrations and spirited confrontations, the war which would become known as the American Revolution began at Lexington and Concord in 1775. There the local militia (citizen soldiers) challenged British soldiers and, as the poet wrote, "fired the shot heard round the world."

Representatives of the thirteen colonies voted to raise troops and George Washington of Virginia was selected as commander-in-chief. The initial intention of the Americans was to acquire the rights which they felt were due them as British subjects, the most important being the right to representation. The British monarch, King George III, saw the colonists' actions as rebellious and was determined to suppress them.

Although for the next two years fighting was heavy and frequent in northern and the middle colonies, Great Britain had not been able to win the conflict decisively. The British intention was to force a confrontation with George Washington's army and destroy it. However, the Continental Army, besieged and battered, had escaped annihilation through two bitter years.

In Great Britain patience with the war was running out. King George III was determined to teach his rebellious subjects a lesson, while the opposition leader to his government, William Pitt (Lord Chatham) warned that continuing the conflict would result in France getting involved. Also there was reason for the King's Prime Minister, Lord North, to be concerned. Taxes had risen tenfold; reports of casualties continued; the expectation that the rebellion would be promptly put down had not been realized. The war raged on: and, short of troops, Great Britain had obtained the services of European rulers, especially German, and was paying for about 30,000 foreign troops (Cook, 1995).

Although the British army had won some victories, they had been humiliated at Lexington, Breed's Hill, and Trenton. Lord North, with the King's approval (Cook, 1995), made inquiries about the possibility of the cessation of hostilities with the colonists. When the colonists insisted on independence, there was little hope of peace. The King flatly refused to consider it and, in doing so, prolonged the war for another four years (Cook, 1995).

In the summer of 1777, a British army under the command of General John Burgoyne had moved down from Canada with the intention of capturing Albany and, consequently, confronting George Washington and putting down the 'rebellion'. At the Battle of Bennington, 16 August 1777, Burgoyne lost a quarter of his German troops, lost over 100 of the local Loyalists who had joined the British, and had been deserted by the Indians who had terrorized the American settlers.

Then, 19 September 1777, Burgoyne suffered staggering casualties, almost seven hundred in one day, at Freeman's Farm. Most of these casualties were British regulars,

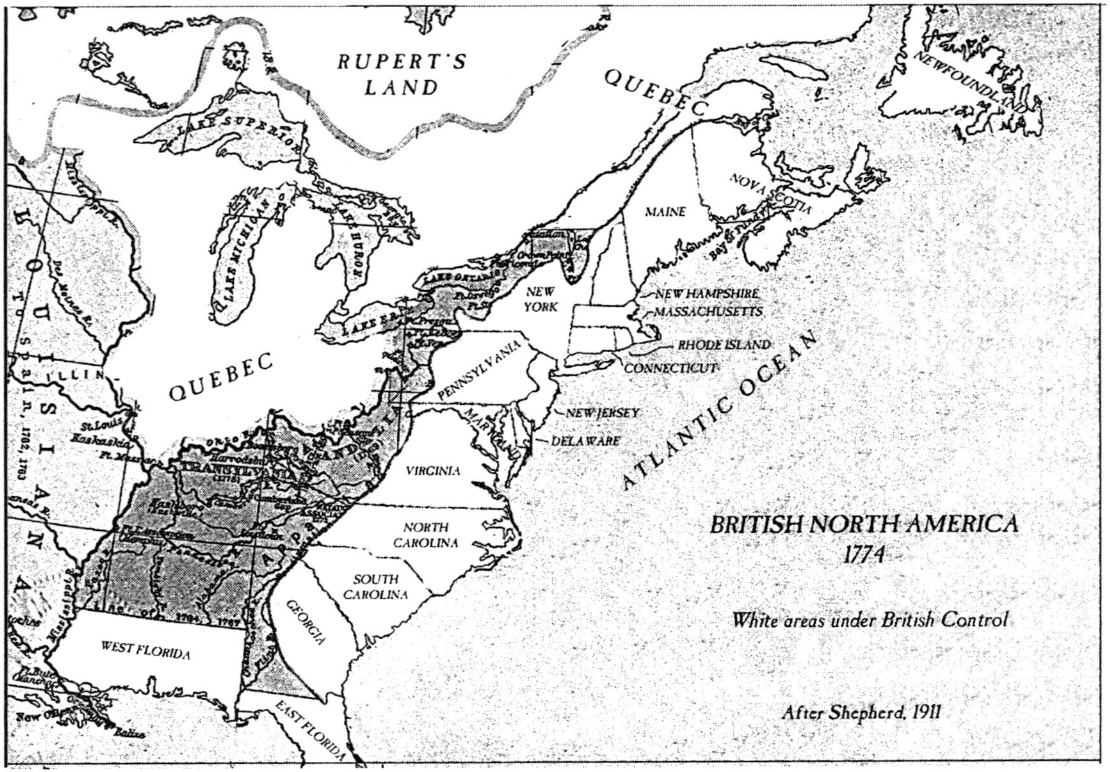
BRITISH NORTH AMERICA
1774
White areas under British Control
After Shepherd, 1911
RUPERT'S LAND
QUEBEC
QUEBEC
NEWFOUNDLAND
NOVA SCOTIA
MAINE
NEW HAMPSHIRE
MASSACHUSETTS
RHODE ISLAND
CONNECTICUT
NEW YORK
NEW JERSEY
DELAWARE
PENNSYLVANIA
MARYLAND
VIRGINIA
NORTH CAROLINA
SOUTH CAROLINA
GEORGIA
EAST FLORIDA
WEST FLORIDA
ATLANTIC OCEAN
LAKE SUPERIOR
LAKE MICHIGAN
LAKE HURON
LAKE ERIE
LAKE ONTARIO
TRANSYLVANIA
LOUISIANA
To Spain, 1762, 1763
St. Louis
Kaskaskia
Des Moines R.
Mississippi R.
New Orleans
Balize

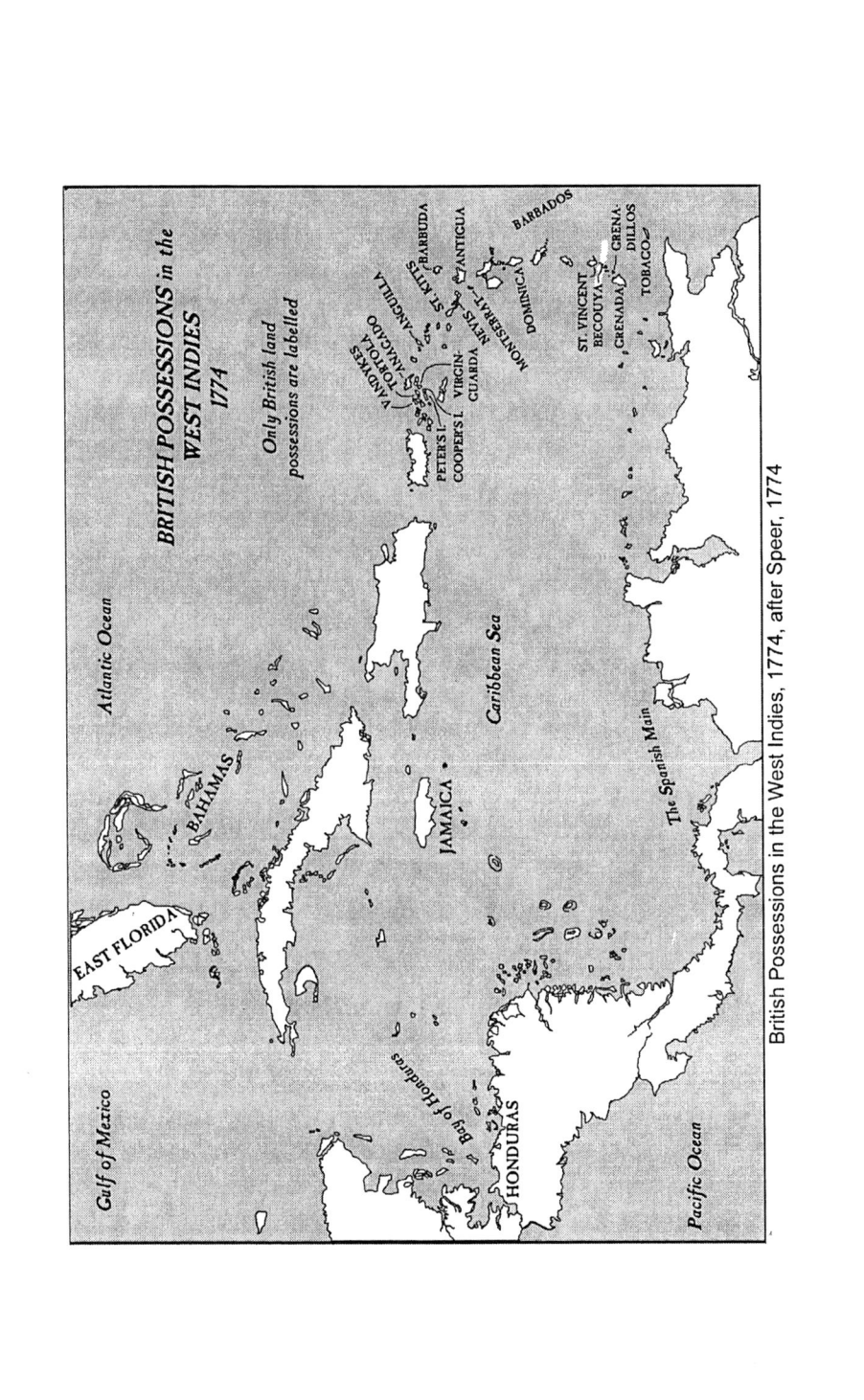

British Possessions in the West Indies, 1774, after Speer, 1774

officers and soldiers, and had been targeted by American riflemen commanded by Colonel Daniel Morgan. Finally, Burgoyne was forced to surrender the remains of his army on 17 October 1777 (Murray, 1998). This loss of about 4,000 troops (Lumpkin, 1981) had repercussions in the British Parliament. The present situation in America would require far more men if there was any hope of keeping the colonies. The best estimate at the time was for an increase of thirty thousand soldiers in America. Some suggested one hundred thousand would not be enough. The British army was already stretched across the Empire. France was now recognizing the colonies and had promised support. Holland also recognized the colonists. The ongoing conflict with Spain for control of the New World meant that British troops were widely dispersed over their vast empire. Another solution was sought (Cook, 1995).

While Lord Chatham argued for an end to the conflict, King George III was adamant that the colonists should be punished. He had as his instrument, Lord George Germain, the Secretary for the American Department, who was determined to crush the rebellion (Cook, 1995). Although many, including Lord North, probably realized that the war could not be won on Britain's terms, there was no hope of convincing the King.

Lord Germain, with the King's approval, initiated what we now call the Southern Campaign or Southern Strategy. Always believing that most colonists were loyal to their King and merely misled by a few rebellious New Englanders, the British now turned their attention to the southern colonies. The plan was to take troops from the north and attack the south. There, it was believed, the loyal citizens would rise up and support the British Army and the territory would be won. Then, triumphant, the British troops would march to the north and defeat George Washington. These Loyalists, or Tories, would solve Britain's manpower problem. This

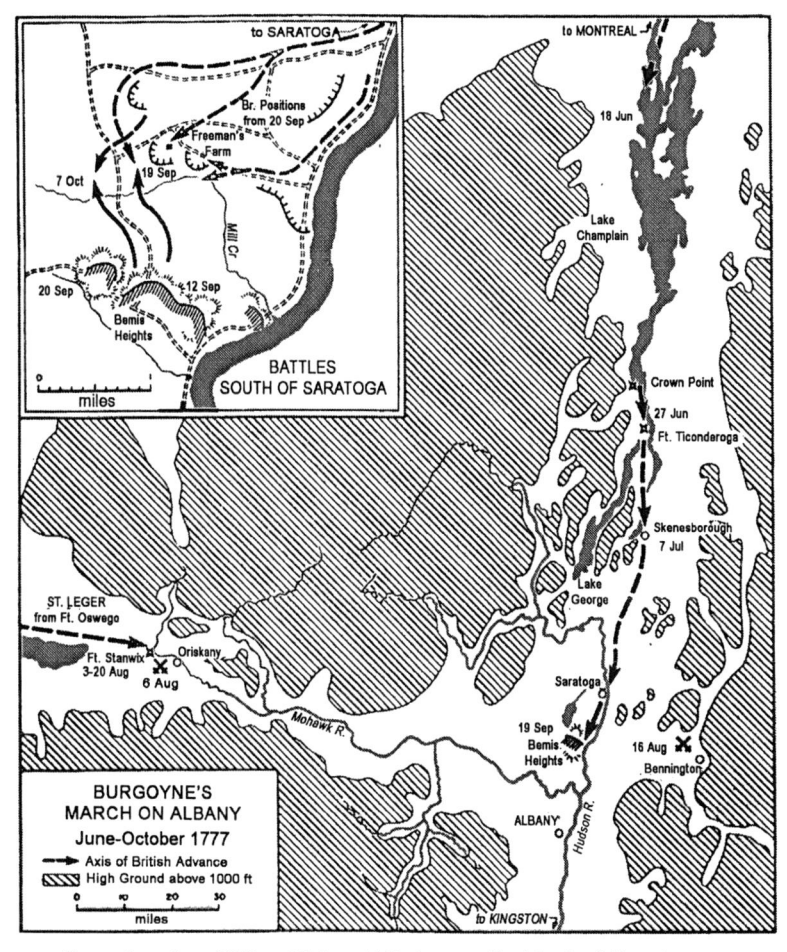

From *American Military History*, U.S. Army, edited for legibility of text.

would 'Americanize' the war.

However, there was another argument used to persuade the reluctant members of Parliament. At the beginning of the Industrial Revolution Britain was the greatest producer in the world (Stokesbury, 1991). They not only did not need industrial New England, but many merchants and ship owners saw that area as competition.

> An empire in North America which consisted of Hudson's Bay, Newfoundland, Quebec and Nova Scotia in the north, the Atlantic seaboard from the Chesapeake capes to Florida, and the British West Indian islands in the south, was not to be despised, and would be a reasonable solution to Britain's difficulties. Feeling the birth pangs of the Industrial Revolution, Britain did not really need the irreconcilably rebellious northern colonies, and might well be better off without them. If the north were lost, so be it. If the south were salvageable, then it should be done soon. (Stokesbury, 1991: 195-196).

There is certainly no evidence that the King or Lord Germain would have considered anything less than complete victory over all the colonies, but the argument had appeal to many of the members of the House of Commons whose profits were plummeting because of the colonists' refusal to import from England. Shipping interests also saw the wisdom of targeting the great wealth of South Carolina, a source of the indigo and rice trade (Edgar, 1998). The virgin forests of the south would provide naval stores and lumber needed for a navy of wooden ships. Further, the rich plantations in the south, with slave labor, could supply food, especially rice, for the slaves on the sugar plantations in the British West Indies. Sugar, rum and molasses from the islands were a source of great wealth for Great Britain. This

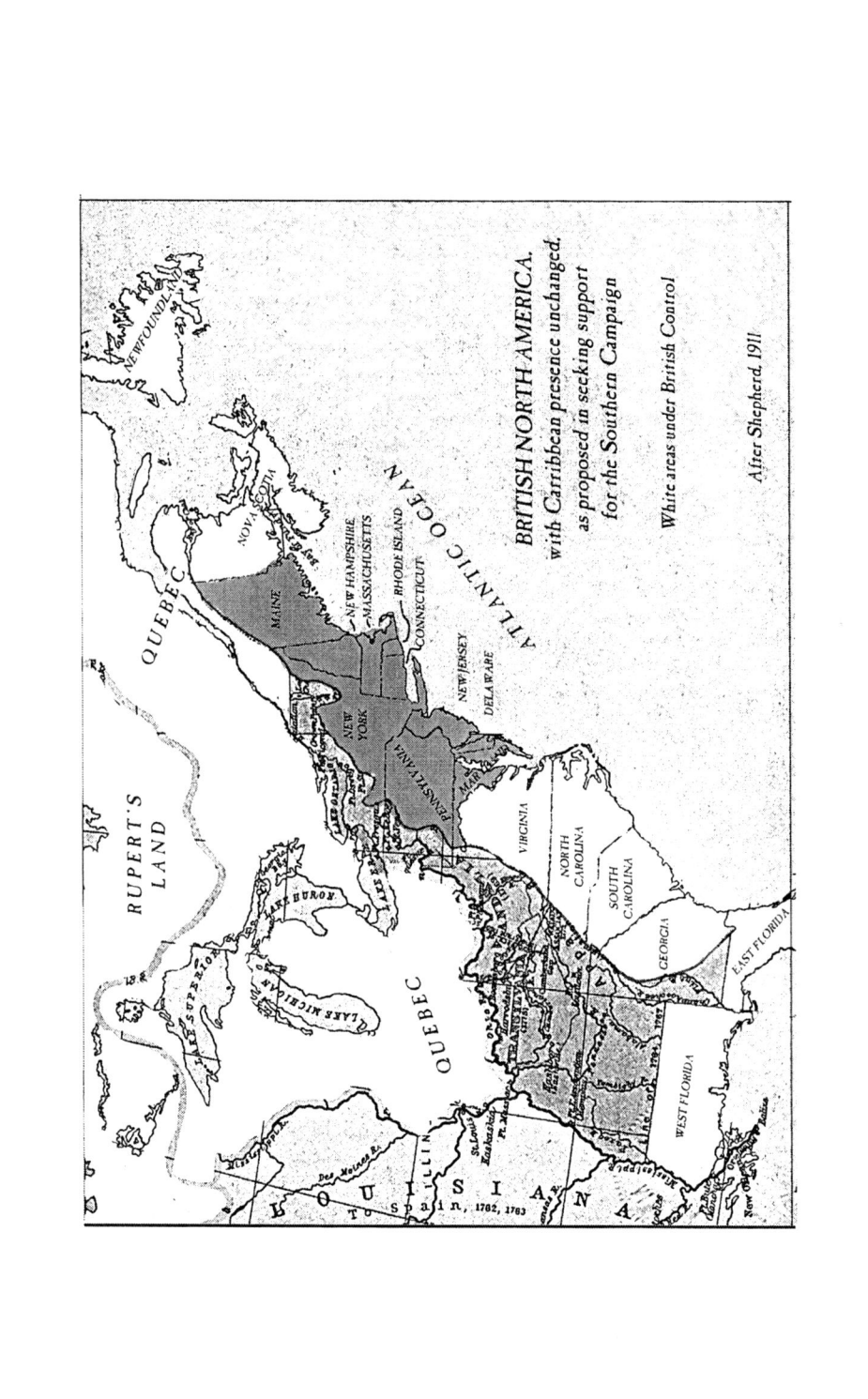

BRITISH NORTH AMERICA.
with Carribbean presence unchanged,
as proposed in seeking support
for the Southern Campaign

White areas under British Control

After Shepherd, 1911

was far less than the King wanted but the argument garnered enough votes from 'back benchers' in the parliament that the government got sufficient support for the Southern Campaign (Stokesbury, 1991).

After an abortive attempt to take Charleston by attacking fortifications on Sullivan's Island (now Fort Moultrie) in June of 1776, the British had concentrated their effort in the north. In December of 1778 British troops occupied Savannah and now Georgia was once again a Royal colony. However, South Carolina had not been brought under British control.

In January of 1780 the new Southern Campaign was underway. The commander of British forces in America, Sir Henry Clinton, and Lord Cornwallis arrived in the Savannah area with 14,000 soldiers, sailors and marines (Stokesbury, 1991). Their destination was Charleston. After a siege of approximately six weeks, Charleston was surrendered to the British on 12 May 1780 (Borick, 2003). The loss of 3,465 men of the Continental army was disastrous to the patriot cause (Borick, 2003). The British imprisoned the Continental soldiers but gave paroles to the militia captured at Charleston. In being paroled the person pledged to no longer pursue the war against the King's forces.

With Charleston won, Sir Henry returned to New York.

> Without much confidence, he turned over the operation in the south to Cornwallis, admonishing him to act prudently, preserve what had been gained at Charleston, and work to restore Loyalist rule. He particularly warned Cornwallis not to outrun his supply lines if he were to move north into Virginia. He left Cornwallis with four thousand men and the independent command he had longed for. (Cook,

The SIEGE of
CHARLESTOWN
1780

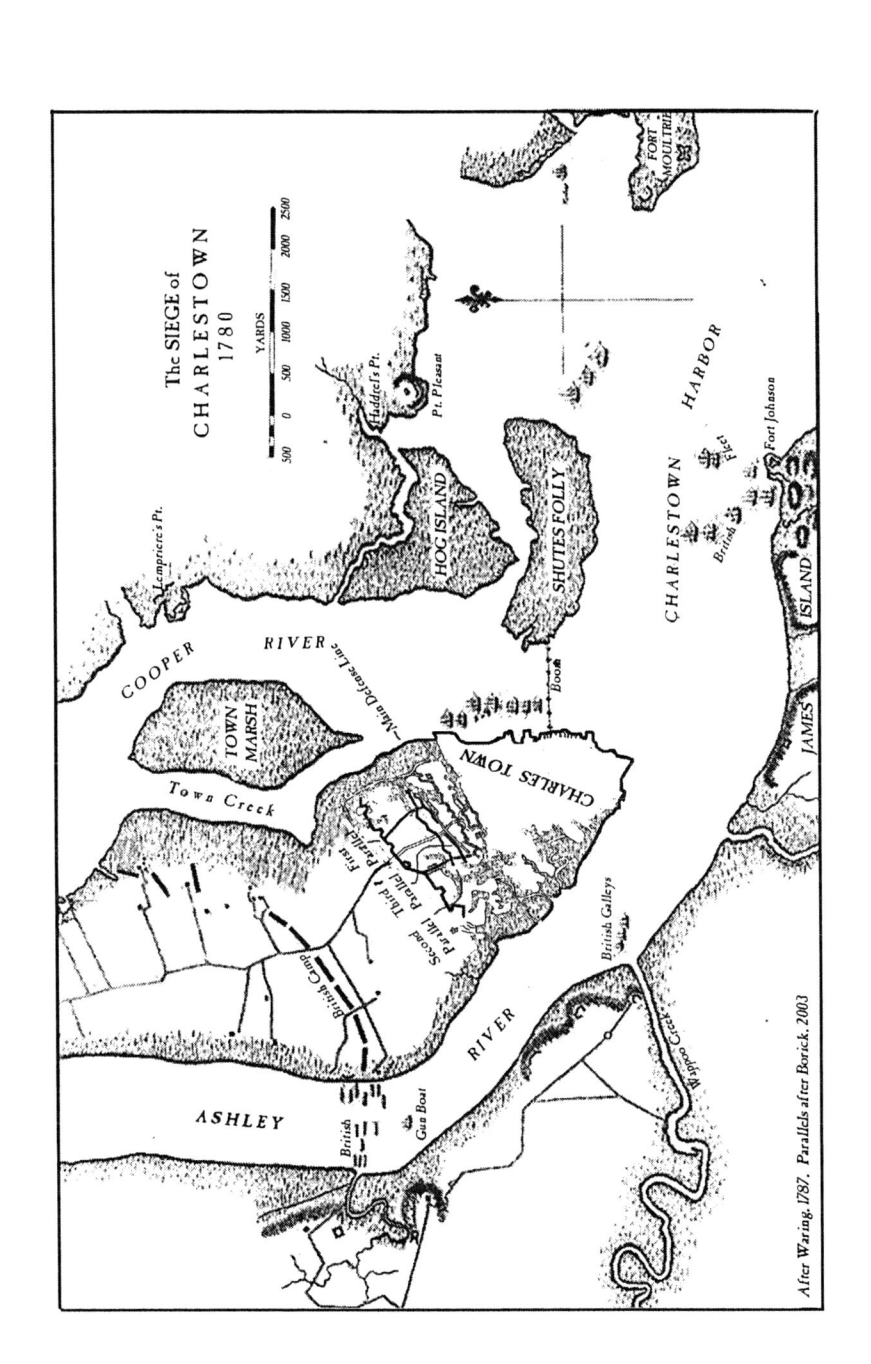

1995: 321).

Before Clinton left South Carolina on 5 June 1780 he had sent detachments to secure outposts around the state:

> They stretched from Georgetown on the coast, up the Pee Dee River to Cheraw, then to Camden, Hanging Rock, and Rocky Mount on to the Catawba-Wateree, on to Ninety-Six near the Saluda, and finally to Augusta, Georgia on the Savannah River...they would serve two purposes: first, they would be havens for the Loyalists; second, and even more importantly, they would serve as bases from which the Royal military, including its Tory allies, could conduct punitive operations against those who continued to defy the king and torment their Loyalist neighbors. (Morrill, 1992: 75-76).

On Clinton's return to New York, he took a defensive position to hold New York and Rhode Island believing he no longer had the troop strength to hunt and destroy George Washington's army (Shy, 1990). With Clinton no longer in an offensive mode, the pressure on George Washington's army was diminished as Clinton remained in New York and Lord Cornwallis campaigned in South Carolina.

Although General Clinton was the commander of the British forces in America, Lord Cornwallis had powerful friends in the British government. He corresponded directly with them and with Lord Germain about his plans for his great campaign which he was sure would end the war.

Neither Lord Germain nor King George III had any idea of the country which Cornwallis now had to secure: not its terrain, its weather or its people. Cornwallis' optimism was what they wished to hear so he had their support. Also,

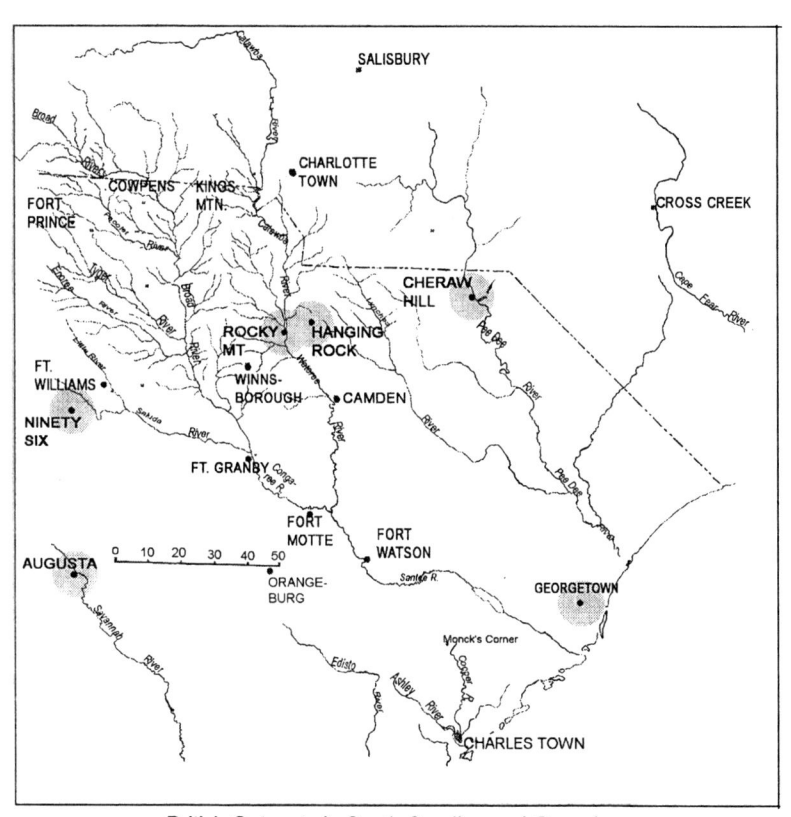

British Outposts in South Carolina and Georgia

the King and Lord Germain wanted to punish the colonists and they trusted Lord Cornwallis to do that. He was an experienced military officer with the reputation as a ferocious fighter and the King was in a fighting mood. Further, Lord Cornwallis appeared to be the exception among military officers at the time in that he cared deeply about the men who served with him. In return, he elicited great loyalty from his troops. However, no one then knew what great sacrifices would be required of the soldiers who remained with Lord Cornwallis.

Many prominent South Carolinians now took paroles believing that further resistance was futile. At first, the parole stipulated that the person would no longer pursue the war against the King's forces, but did not require that the parolee take arms against his neighbors. That was shortly changed by General Clinton before he left South Carolina. He issued a proclamation requiring the parolee to swear allegiance to the King and to bear arms in his service (Buchanan, 1997). Believing that the British had not kept their word, many who had taken parole felt that they were under no obligation as the requirements for parole had changed.

Although the colony of South Carolina was 'occupied' by the British, it was far from conquered. The British Parliament was confident that the King's loyal subjects would now prevail. Nothing was farther from the truth, and much of the blame can be laid on Cornwallis (Edgar, 2001). He had in his command a few 'loose cannons' and one was Lt. Col. Banastre Tarleton. Tarleton and his troopers had sabered to death prisoners at Monck's Corner and at the Waxhaws. Patriots referred to him as 'Bloody Ban' or 'Butcher,' and he was the most hated and feared British soldier in the colony. "Courtesy and honour is for equals, which is not how the rebels were regarded" (Hayter, 2003:129).

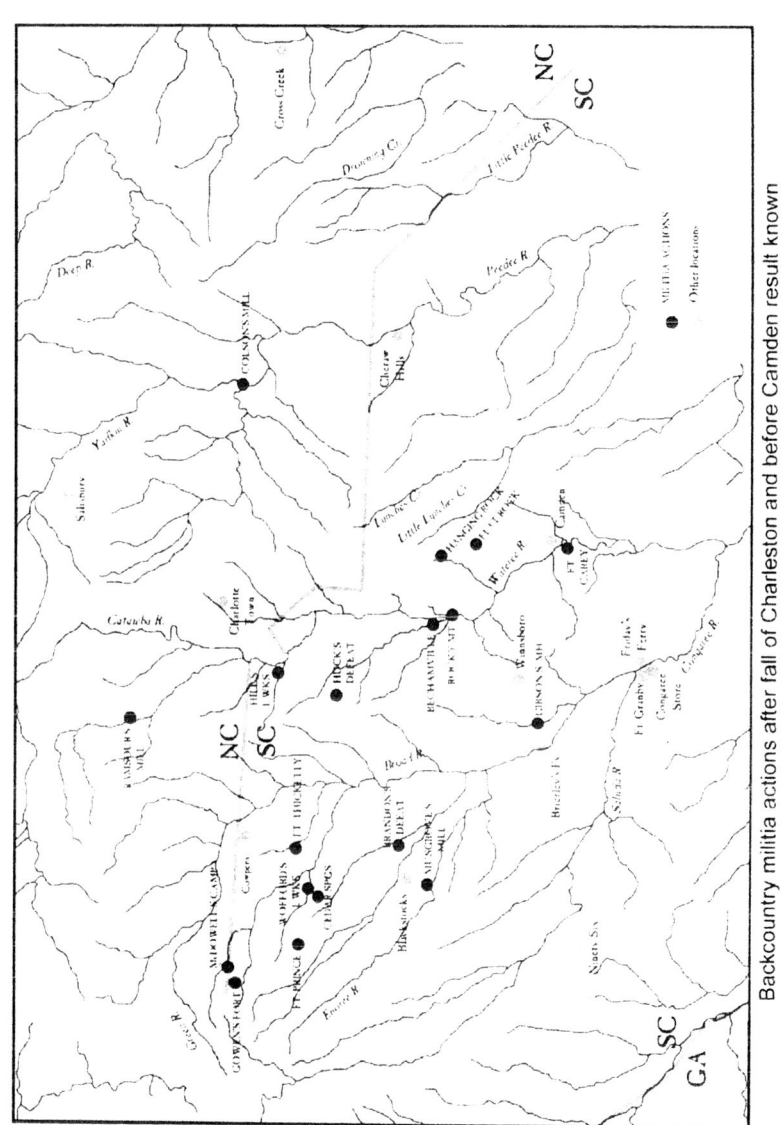

Backcountry militia actions after fall of Charleston and before Camden result known

Tarleton regarded the colonists as beneath contempt and his solution was to annihilate as many as possible. Any thought that the inhabitants could accept such treatment should have been obvious to Cornwallis, but Tarleton was his personal favorite and the outrages were overlooked even when British regular officers such as Ferguson objected (Fortescue, 1911).

The back country was up in arms. Resistance sprang up across the area: Ramsour's Mill in North Carolina (20 June 1780): In South Carolina, Williamson's Plantation, (12 July 1780), where Christian Huck of Tarleton's British Legion was killed; Cedar Springs, (12 July 1780), where Loyalists were ambushed; Gowen's Old Fort, (13 July 1780); Rocky Mount, (30 July 1780); Hanging Rock I, (30 July 1780); Hanging Rock II, (6 August 1780); Carey's Fort, (15 August 1780). (Lumpkin, 1981; O'Kelley, I, 2004).

Another Continental Army, commanded by Major General Horatio Gates, the American hero of Saratoga, arrived in South Carolina, and confronted Cornwallis at Camden on 16 August 1780. (See Endnote 1). Although the Continental soldiers fought bravely, the militia, unaccustomed to the bayonet attacks of British soldiers, panicked and fled the field. The defeat of the American forces was complete and the result, disastrous.

Lord Cornwallis now felt no threat from the Continental Army and had little fear of the militia, which had been swept from the field at Camden, many without firing a shot. Certainly Lord Cornwallis must have felt invincible. He had shown that he could win in the field in conventional warfare but there was another kind of warfare in the back country. Once again, there was no Continental army in South Carolina and the inhabitants were on their own. This would be a different kind of war. The rout of British regulars at Musgrove's Mill (18 August 1789) was another indication of what was in store for Cornwallis although he

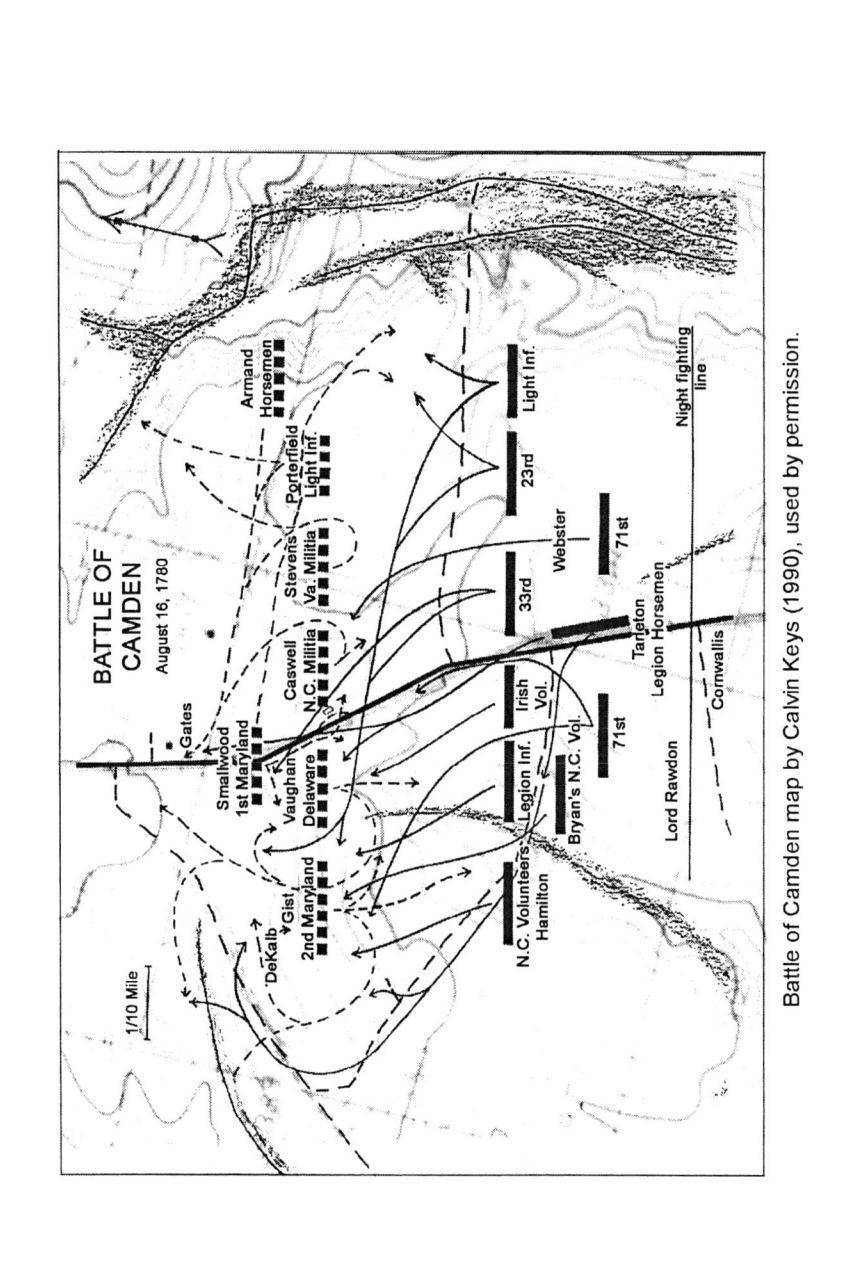

Battle of Camden map by Calvin Keys (1990), used by permission.

chose to ignore the signs (Edgar, 2001).

Cornwallis might have given pause at this point had he been the kind of officer who thought of anything other than the direct assault. In the skirmishes around the area he had lost 500 men, mostly Loyalists, killed or wounded (Pancake, 1985). Before the Battle of Camden there were 800 soldiers in hospital in that town too sick to fight. Also, a battalion of Highlanders posted at Cheraw were so ill that they had to be evacuated. In spite of his great victory at Camden, Cornwallis had lost one in five of his redcoats, killed or wounded, in fierce fighting with the Maryland and Delaware Continentals (Pancake, 1985).

To further complicate matters, after the Battle of Camden, when Cornwallis was feeling secure enough to contemplate a move towards Virginia, Lt. Col. Francis Marion took command of the Williamsburg militia and extended the conflict into the area along the Santee River.

The main road from the port at Charleston to the British post at Camden followed the Santee River and its tributaries and provided the route that the British used to move their supplies. Marion moved along the flood plains of the Santee, Wateree and Pee Dee Rivers and interrupted the flow of British reinforcements and supplies. In the next year, commanders at Camden would send five British officers into the swamps to try to dislodge him, but Marion held no territory for them to attack. When danger threatened, he and his men just faded away into the deep recesses of almost impenetrable swamps. Cornwallis failed to heed Clinton's admonition not to outrun his supply lines as he moved north. His supply lines south of Camden were already in peril.

Cornwallis, his eyes set on Virginia, moved to Charlotte Courthouse (Charlotte, North Carolina) leaving the command of the troops in Camden to Lord Rawdon who was posted there. Lord Cornwallis believed that the situation in South Carolina was under control. Suddenly, he was

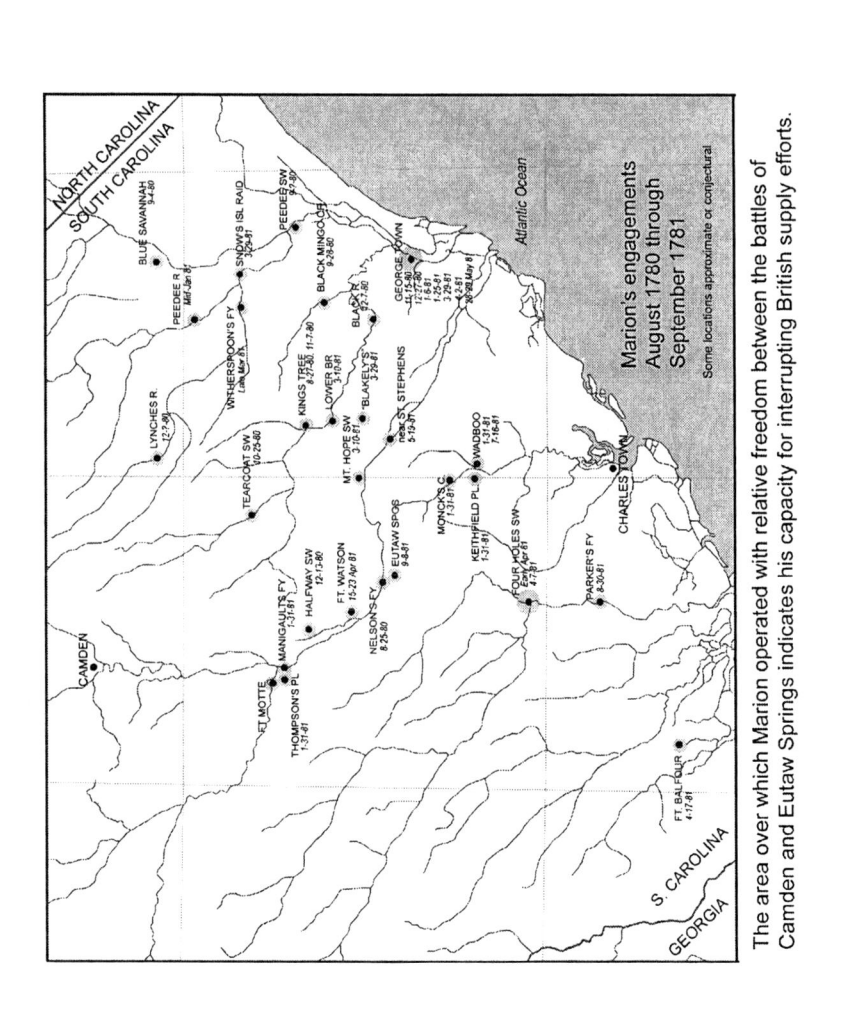

The area over which Marion operated with relative freedom between the battles of Camden and Eutaw Springs indicates his capacity for interrupting British supply efforts.

confronted with the reality of the situation.

Before he had left Carolina, Clinton had appointed Major Patrick Ferguson Inspector of Militia with the task of organizing Loyalist militia in the back county. Ferguson was a competent, professional soldier, who had earned his rank as an officer in the 71st Regiment of Foot, Fraser's Highlanders.

As he had been directed, Ferguson organized a group of 'Ferguson's Rangers', men from the New Jersey and New York Volunteers posted at Ninety-Six. With this cadre he had trained a group of Loyalist (Tory) militia and had moved into the area bordering North and South Carolina. Eager to pacify the interior, he issued an ultimatum to the settlers beyond the mountains in the area which is now Tennessee. They were to come and pledge their support to the King or he would march on them and, with fire and sword, lay waste their settlements.

The men who were threatened were living in Indian territory. They were a hardy, ferocious group who had fought for their survival in a hostile environment. Many, under Col. Isaac Shelby's command, had already confronted and defeated British provincials at Musgrove's Mill. They were determined that Ferguson would not come to their settlements but they would stop him first.

After a march over the mountains, joined by militia from the back country, these men whom we call Over Mountain Men assembled at Cowpens. They then rode to King's Mountain where, they discovered, Ferguson was encamped with about 100 provincial soldiers and 900 Tories.

On 7 October 1780 the mountaineers assaulted the forces of Major Ferguson (O'Kelley, 2004). It was long rifles against muskets and bayonets. It was aimed fire against volley fire. It was frontier warfare and the backwoodsmen won. Ferguson was killed and his troops killed, wounded, or taken prisoners. Some prisoners, who were locals who had meted harsh treatment on their patriot neighbors, were hanged; the rest moved north as prisoners (Lumpkin, 1981).

When Cornwallis was informed of the loss of Ferguson he realized that the militia, which he could sweep from the field in a set battle, posed a serious problem. Although he had the utmost contempt for the American militia he now saw the threat.

To continue to move to the north, Lord Cornwallis would be leaving Ninety-Six and Camden exposed. He moved his headquarters back to Winnsboro, South Carolina. Cornwallis, himself, was ill and had to be transported in a wagon. Many of his soldiers suffered from yellow fever, malaria, and camp fever, diseases which debilitated his forces. He hoped for a winter camp at Winnsboro where he and his troops could recuperate. It was not to be.

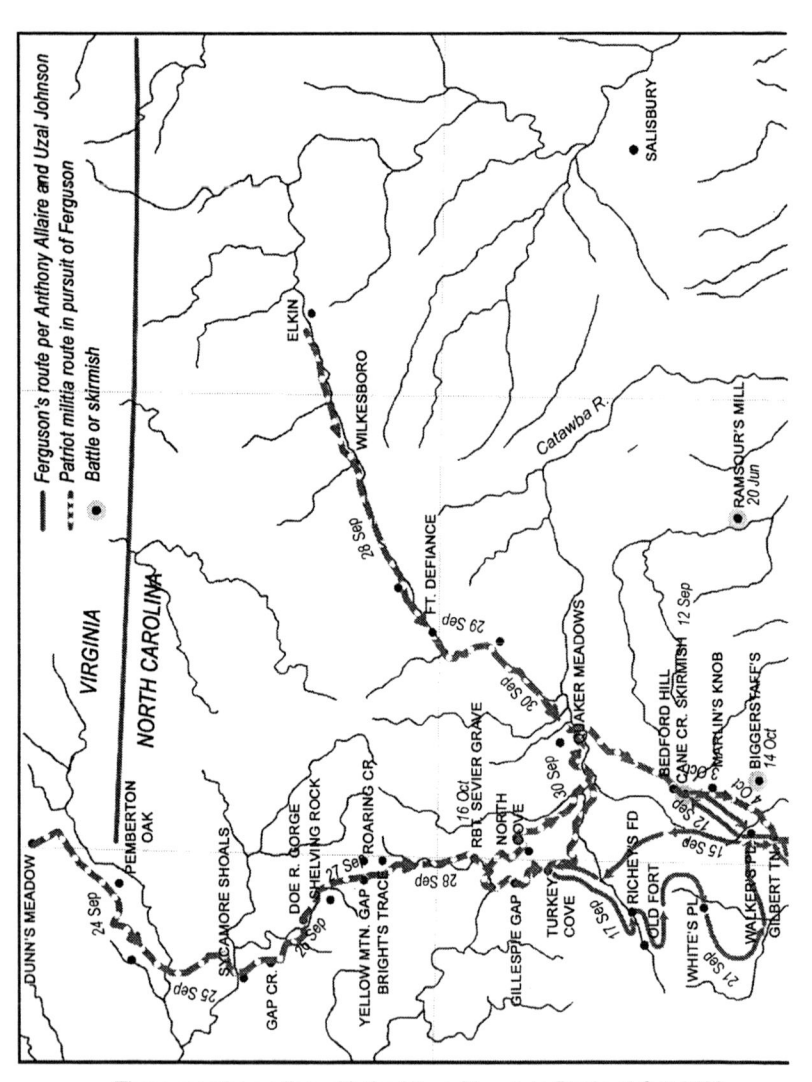

Three months ending with the Kings Mountain Battle, 7 Oct 1780

with movements of the opposing forces and with engagements in the area.

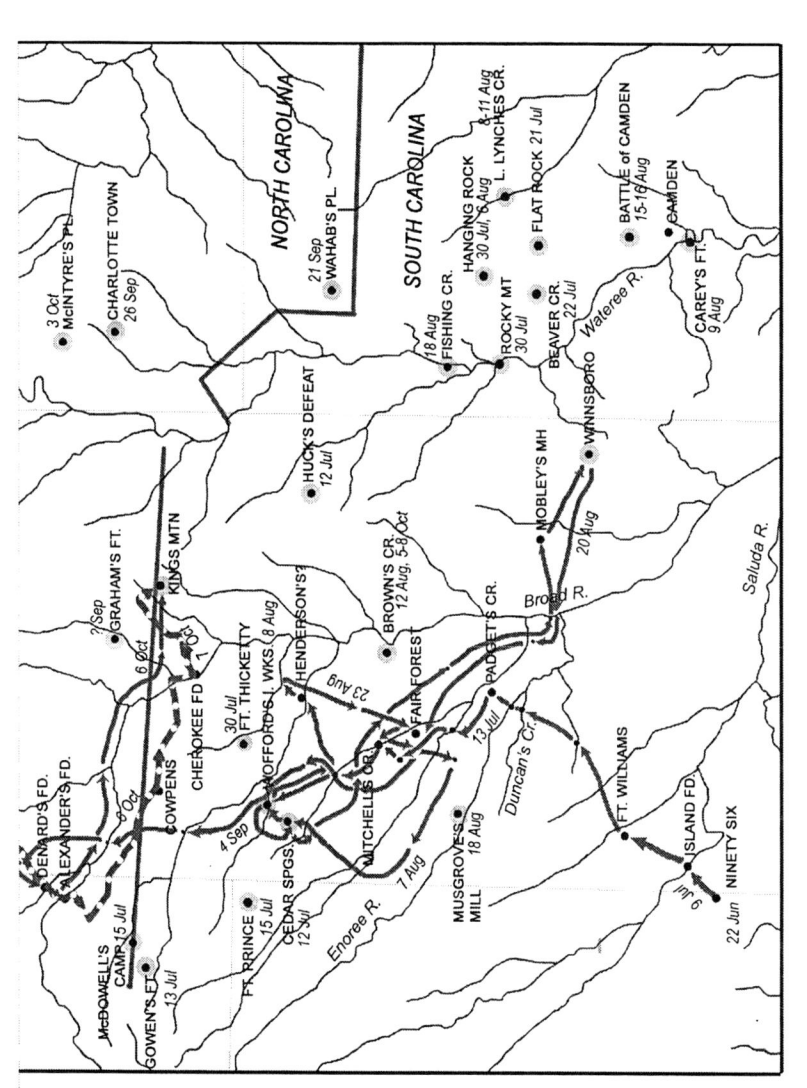

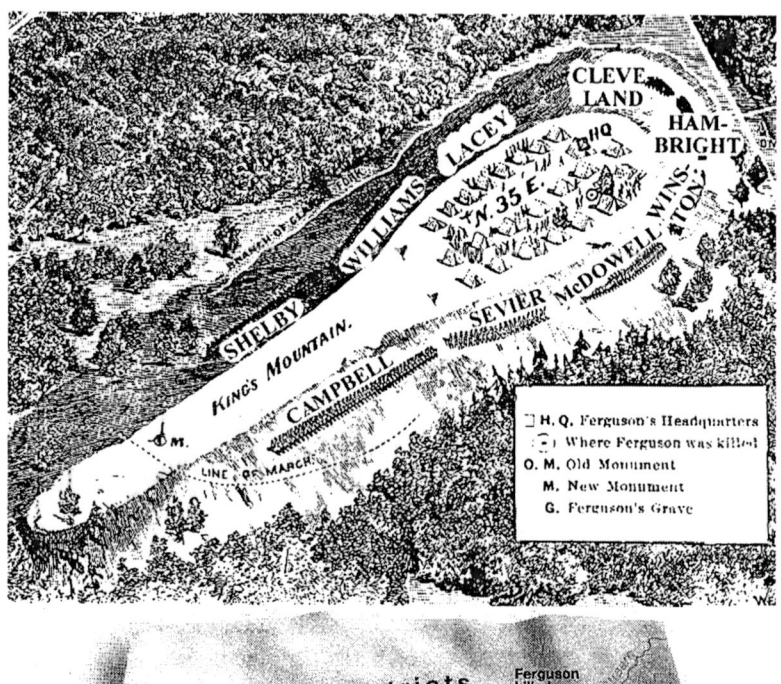

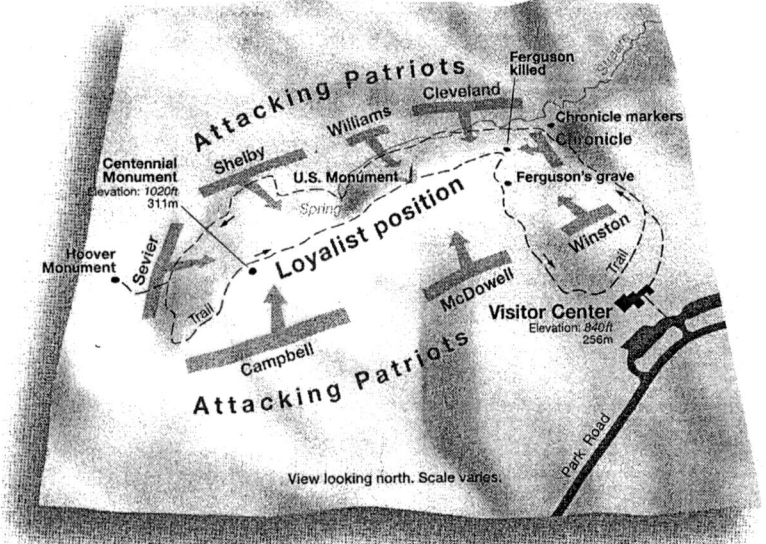

Maps of Kings Mountain show varying positions for the Patriot militia forces. Differences can be seen between Draper's 1881 map and that shown in a modern NPS Kings Mountain NMP brochure.

CHAPTER II

TROUBLE IN THE BACK COUNTRY

The Continental Army in the South had been in shambles after the Battle of Camden in August. Those soldiers who had not been killed or captured had escaped to Hillsboro, North Carolina, where Major General Gates tried to hold his shattered army together and regroup. Congress was slow in recognizing the need to supply this army but General of the Army George Washington saw the need for a strong presence in the South in view of the threat posed by Lord Cornwallis.

Congress had appointed the three commanders in the south. The first had lost an army at Savannah, the second had lost an army at Charleston, and the third had been routed at Camden. Congress had lost confidence in Major General Horatio Gates and General Washington would have the opportunity of selecting a replacement. He chose Major General Nathanael Greene and things would change in the Southern Campaign. Here was the man who would lead his army through the south and command at Eutaw Springs.

At first glance, Nathanael Greene might seem an odd choice for such a daunting task. In an American Army where most senior officers had previous service with British troops during the French and Indian Wars (1756-1763), Greene had no military service prior to the American Revolution.

Born into a Quaker family in 1742, Nathanael Greene was deprived of a first-rate education by a father who believed that one need only be literate enough to read the Scriptures (F. V. Greene, 1893). However, the Greene family was prosperous, owning a forge, grist mill, flour mill, saw mill and mercantile store. Young Greene learned the value of hard work in his family's businesses. As he prospered, he bought books and acquired a considerable library. Feeling the lack of his liberal education, he read widely and sought the company of literate companions.

Although self-taught, Greene was reputed to have a superior mind and a Herculean memory (Johnson, 1822). It was written of him:

> He was never considered by his associates as an uneducated man; ....Above all, he had a clear mental vision and sound judgment. His mind saw realities, and not pictures.
> (F. V. Greene, 1893:9)

When it was obvious to him that the dispute with England could not be solved amicably, Nathanael Greene purchased a musket and joined the militia. In spite of being instrumental in forming the unit, he was not selected as an officer, possibly because he limped due to a stiff knee.

In May 1775, Rhode Island decided to raise an army of fifteen hundred men and Nathanael Greene was elected by the Assembly as brigadier general in command. By the end of May 1775, the army was en route to Boston to join George Washington. (See Endnote 2).

When Washington and Greene met in July of 1775, there was a friendship cemented which would last through the difficult war years. Washington was impressed with the intelligence and integrity of the young general, and Greene was totally committed from that time forward to furthering Washington's agenda. At the end of the war, of all the commanding officers who were assembled in Boston, only Greene remained in active command. Nowhere in Greene's extensive correspondence is the slightest hint of any disregard for his Commander-in-Chief.

When Congress pressed for a replacement for General Gates, Washington appointed Greene. Although Washington involved Greene in every battle he commanded in the northern theater, the general from Rhode Island was still comparatively inexperienced compared to the British commander he would face. However, Greene was considered to be able to perform under fire, to act decisively and to move troops expeditiously. And, in the north, he had twice thwarted Lord Cornwallis on the field of battle. He also had made contacts with officers such as William Washington and Daniel Morgan who would figure prominently in Greene's new command.

As Greene moved south he gleaned all the information he could about the terrain, the rivers, the militia personnel, and the plight of the southern army. One bright note in his journey was the news of Patrick Ferguson's defeat at King's Mountain at the hands of the back country militia.

His service as quartermaster had taught Greene the importance of terrain for camps and the movement of supplies. As Greene sent detachments to measure the depth and current of the rivers he would need to move supplies, he ordered axes and saws, boat nails, horseshoes and wagons. He knew what it would take to move an army.

Although Greene had long advocated the need for a strong Continental Army, that need was not being met by Congress. Militia would have to be used. It was fortunate that Greene had, in the south, some exceptionally competent militia leaders who had been successful in disrupting the British presence: Thomas Sumter, Francis Marion, Andrew Pickens and Elijah Clarke had been active. The Over Mountain Men under Sevier, Shelby. Cleveland, Lacey and McDowell had defeated Ferguson. Greene corresponded with many of the militia leaders and was assured of their participation.

Greene traveled to Charlotte and took command of the Continental Army in the south. Now, the struggle would be between Lord Cornwallis, an experienced, competent, career commander, and a cerebral Nathanael Greene. Greene had gathered all the information he could about the area in which he would campaign and he knew more about the geography of the area than Gates had acquired in the several months he had been there. Greene's attention to detail was legendary.

Greene understood the British situation possibly better than the British commander did himself. Lord Cornwallis had suffered a considerable number of casualties; his supply lines were threatened; he could not replace dead and wounded soldiers; and, he was moving even farther from his port at Charleston. The British no longer controlled the road from Charleston to Camden. Lord Cornwallis had sent Lt. Col. Banastre Tarleton into the area in November to attempt to dislodge Francis Marion from the swamps where he threatened the road. Tarleton had failed to neutralize Marion. Now, Greene would capitalize on Marion's ability to control the supply lines north of the Santee River.

Greene had inherited an army which was undermanned, poorly equipped and ill clothed. However, Greene intended to inflict as many casualties as possible on Cornwallis as he rebuilt his own American army. It would be a war of attrition and Greene had the officers who were capable of inflicting such damage.

Col. Otho Holland Williams, who had been serving with Gates, was known to Greene as they had served together in the north. Williams became Greene's adjutant general.

There were other officers with the Southern Army who were experienced and dependable: General Daniel Morgan, Lt. Col. William Washington, Lt. Col. John Eager Howard, and Captain Robert Kirkwood. Greene would utilize the capabilities of these officers immediately.

If Lord Cornwallis wondered at the strategy of the new commander of the Continental Army in the South, he did not have to wait long.

Now Greene, against all military logic, divided his inferior force in the face of a superior army. The next blow to Cornwallis would come in the west as Greene sent Brigadier General Daniel Morgan, the hero of the Battle of Saratoga, westward with some of the best troops Greene had in his army.

While in Boston, Greene had the opportunity to make the acquaintance of the colorful Morgan when the Virginian arrived at Boston Neck with his sharpshooters. Morgan was not of the educated and affluent class which Congress preferred as officers, but was a ferocious fighter and fearless leader.

When the British General Burgoyne moved down from Canada toward Albany, he was accompanied by Indians who were terrorizing the local inhabitants. George Washington knew of Morgan's success as an Indian fighter and sent him to join Gates who was attempting to stop Burgoyne. On 17 September 1777, at the first battle for Saratoga, the Battle at Freeman's Farm, Morgan's riflemen, supported by infantry with bayonets, inflicted almost seven hundred casualties on Burgoyne's army in one day (Murray, 1998). Burgoyne would later comment that his campaign was defeated largely due to the riflemen under the command of Colonel Daniel Morgan as they shot his officers and sergeants and killed the artillerymen as they served their guns. It might not have been what the British thought was gentlemanly conduct, but Daniel Morgan had been trained in the art of survival in the wilderness and Indian territory. He had learned his lessons well.

Morgan's health was precarious. His body suffered from years of exposure and abuse. He had not fought at Camden but had joined Gates at Hillsboro where the remains of the Continental Army were encamped and General Gates was attempting to rebuild. When Lord Cornwallis had retreated from Charlotte Courthouse to Winnsboro, Morgan had moved with the Continental Army to Charlotte Courthouse. It was here that Major General Nathanael Greene took command of the Southern Army and started to implement his strategy.

Greene intended to inflict as many casualties on Lord Cornwallis' army as possible and to thwart the British at every turn. He trusted that Daniel Morgan would do that. Morgan was a man of action. He was a warrior on whom Greene could depend. The British general, John Burgoyne, had learned that Morgan was a worthy adversary. Now Lord Cornwallis would be taught the same lesson.

Although Morgan held a commission as brigadier general in the Continental Army, he was a far different sort than Greene. Morgan was a backwoodsman from western Virginia who had learned that there was no civility in war. He was bold, decisive and steadfast in battle.

Major General Nathanael Greene had the social credentials which Washington wanted in his general officers. Greene was cultured, well-read, intelligent and ambitious. He was a student of military and political history, as well as of warfare. He was also an astute judge of men and he recognized Morgan's worth.

Morgan was a practitioner of war, a battle-scarred veteran who could be depended upon to command with authority and inflict maximum damage on the enemy. Furthermore, the campaign would have to rely on militia and Morgan understood the militia. Greene would give Morgan an independent command which would travel far beyond Greene's control. This fast-moving group would be called the Flying Army.

The Flying Army which Morgan would command included other fine officers in whom Greene had great confidence. Lt. Col. William Washington, a second cousin (once removed) of General George Washington, was one of the officers who accompanied Morgan. Washington was commander of the cavalry which was part of the Flying Army. Washington will remain with Greene and play an important role at Eutaw Springs.

Another officer accompanying Morgan was Lt. Col. John Eager Howard of Maryland. Lt. Col. Howard was another officer on whom Greene could depend for leadership. He will command Morgan's infantry at Cowpens, then serve with Greene for the rest of the campaign. He will command troops at Eutaw Springs.

Captain Robert Kirkwood of Delaware was another officer who had distinguished himself under fire. He would accompany Morgan to Cowpens, then join Greene for the remainder of the campaign and play an important role at Eutaw Springs.

Not only would these officers provide leadership to Greene's Southern Command, but also would provide valuable intelligence. Greene was known to research every aspects of the war and the conduct of his enemy. The knowledge he would gain from the men who had faced Lord Cornwallis at Camden, and had fought the dreaded Lt. Col. Tarleton, would be crucial.

Now, on 16 December 1780, Brigadier General Daniel Morgan and his Flying Army were ordered west into the area close to the South Carolina-North Carolina border. His mission was to spirit up the patriots and to annoy the enemy.

Morgan's Flying Army consisted of Continental infantry from Maryland, Delaware, Virginia and North Carolina.

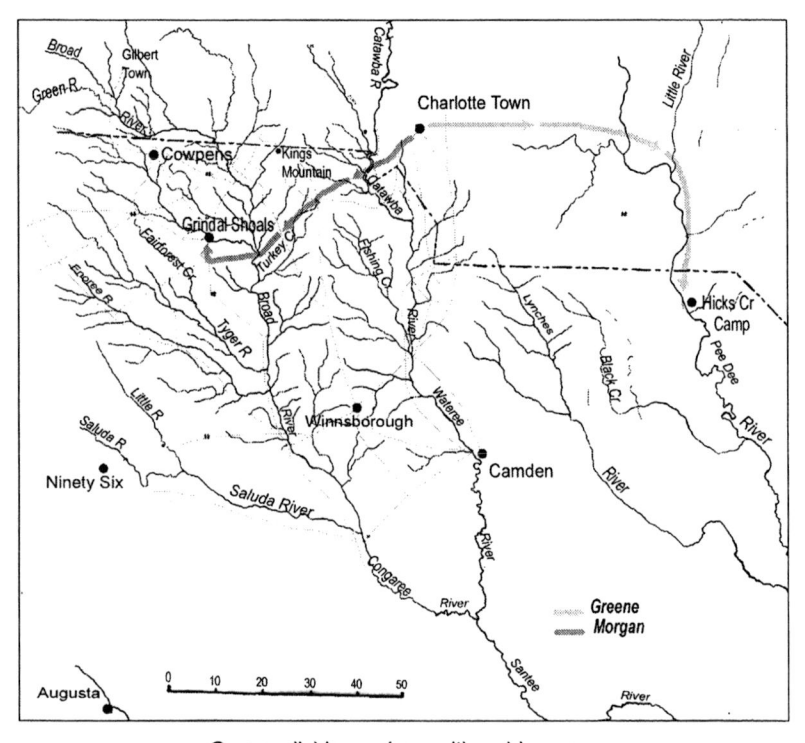

Greene divides and repositions his army

They were accompanied by Virginia State Troops and Virginia militia (Babits, 1998).

As Morgan moved his troops west, Greene moved the remainder of the army east to the new camp at Hick's Creek. He established a new headquarters on the confluence of the Pee Dee River and Hick's Creek (present day Wallace, South Carolina). It was here that Lt. Col. Henry Lee reported to Major General Nathanael Greene. Unlike Gates before him, Greene saw the value of cavalry, especially in the back country of the south. Lt. Col. Henry Lee and his Legion consisted of about two hundred and eighty men, including both cavalry and infantry (Lee, 1812).

Greene immediately dispatched Lee down the Pee Dee River to campaign with militia leader Francis Marion who continued to harass the British supply lines from Charleston to Camden. Now Marion's Brigade and Lee's Legion would provide a significant American force between the British posts of Camden and Georgetown, as well as between Camden and Charleston.

Lord Cornwallis, aware of Morgan's movement to the west, was faced with the problem arising from General Greene's divided army. If Lord Cornwallis moved to confront General Greene in his position on the Pee Dee River, Morgan would be behind the British Army and threaten British posts at Ninety-Six and Augusta. If Lord Cornwallis pursued Daniel Morgan to the west, General Greene was not only behind the British Army but in a position to strike Camden and/or Charleston. This was a disturbing situation for Lord Cornwallis in Winnsboro and Lord Rawdon who commanded in Camden.

Although the defeat and death of Major Patrick Ferguson at King's Mountain had forced Lord Cornwallis back into South Carolina, he had not abandoned the backcountry. Lt. Col. Banastre Tarleton had been moving through the area and had encountered General Thomas Sumter's militia as

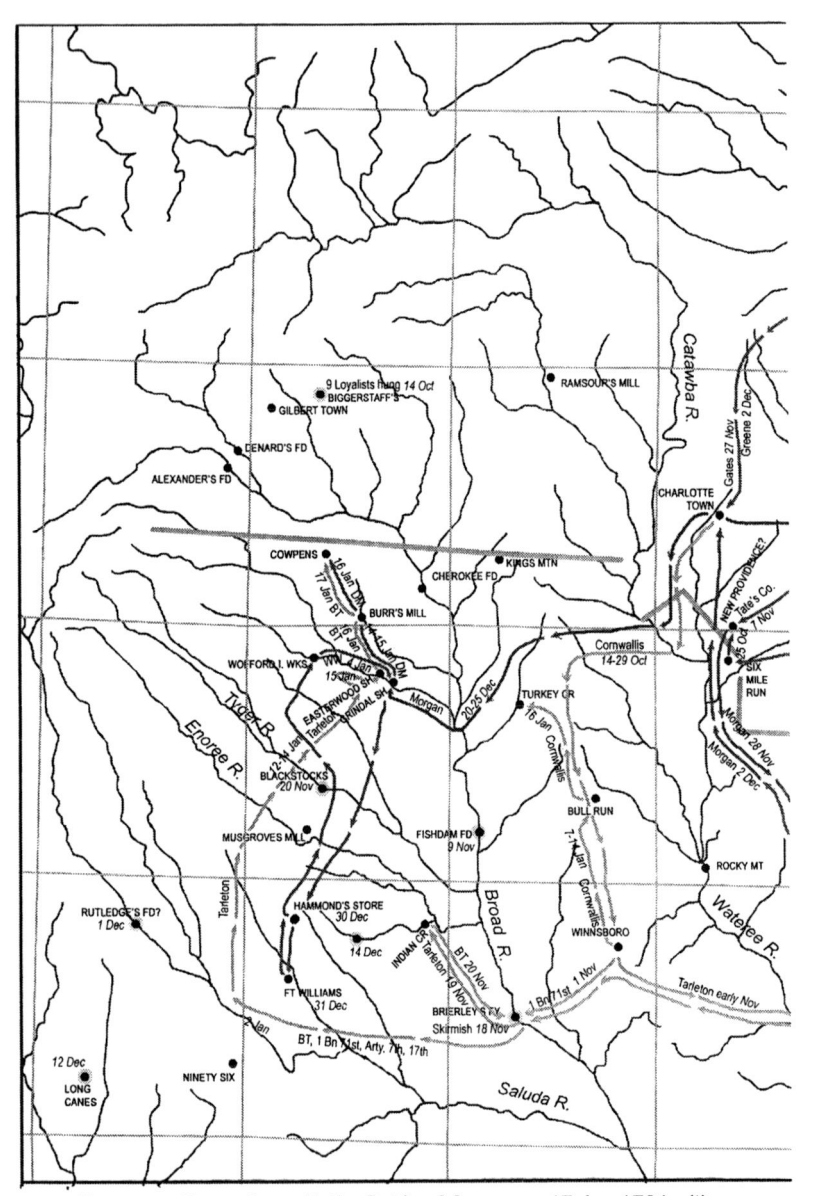

Three months ending with the Battle of Cowpens, 17 Jan 1781, with

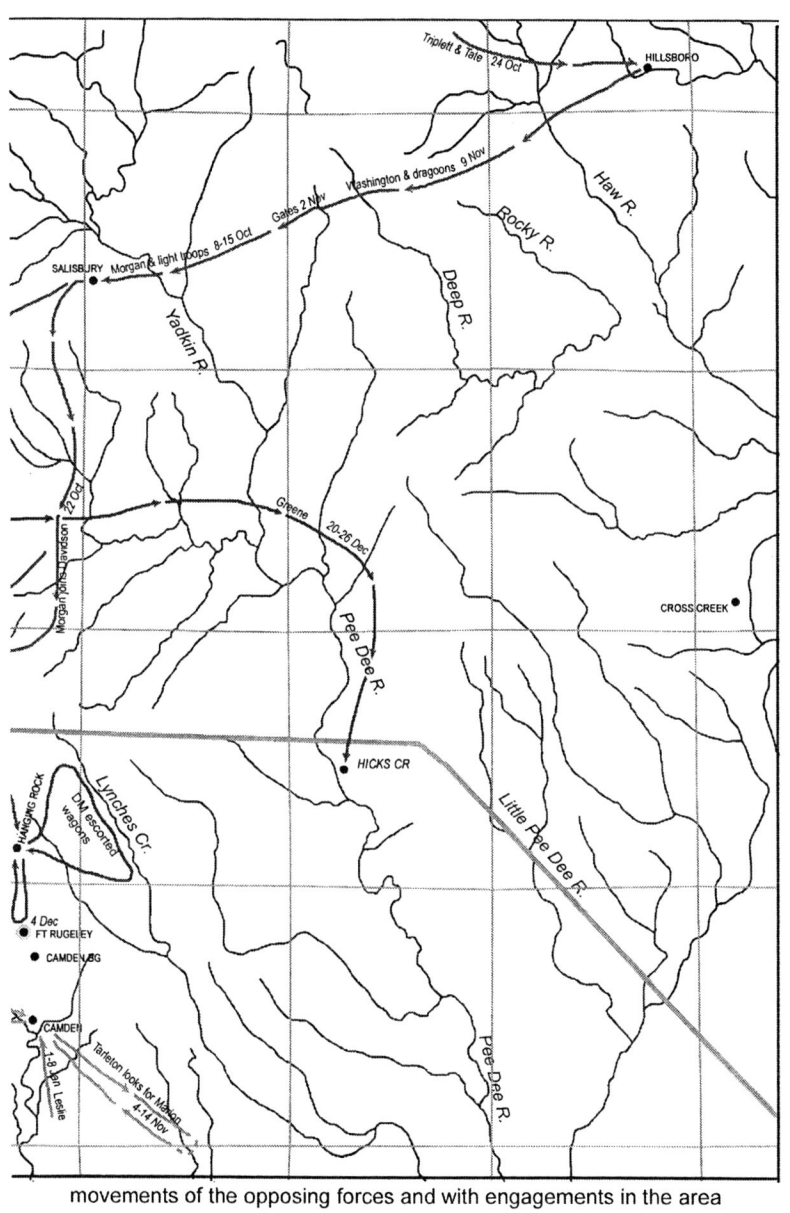

movements of the opposing forces and with engagements in the area

well as Col. Elijah Clarke's militia at Blackstock's Farm. On 20 November, the impetuous Tarleton attacked the fortified patriot position with the loss of almost one hundred British soldiers. Although Tarleton reported this to Lord Cornwallis as a victory (Tarleton, 1787), Sumter's militia suffered only four casualties, including a serious wound to Sumter himself.

Lord Cornwallis continued to monitor the situation without knowing Morgan's intentions or his exact position. However, American cavalry, under the command of Lt. Col. William Washington, and mounted militia, commanded by Major James McCall, annihilated a group of Georgian Tories at Hammond's Store on 30 December 1780. Washington then moved closer to Ninety-Six and captured the British stockade, Fort Williams, which was only fifteen miles from Ninety-Six. Cornwallis had to respond. The Continentals were threatening Ninety-Six, an important British outpost in the back country. Cornwallis sent a force under the command of Lt. Col. Banastre Tarleton to check Morgan.

> For ten days in early January Tarleton first looked for, and then chased Morgan, whom he outnumbered two to one. On January 17 he made the mistake of catching him. (Stokesbury, 1991:237).

The Battle of Cowpens is studied by military services and historians in this country as well as those in other nations. The tactics were innovative and resulted in a double envelopment, one of the few in history. Although Morgan had been successful in many encounters, it is at the battle of Cowpens where he demonstrated his tactical talents, and he may be the best battlefield commander this nation ever produced (Buchanan, 1997).

Morgan had studied Tarleton's behavior in previous events and he knew his enemy. However, Tarleton greatly

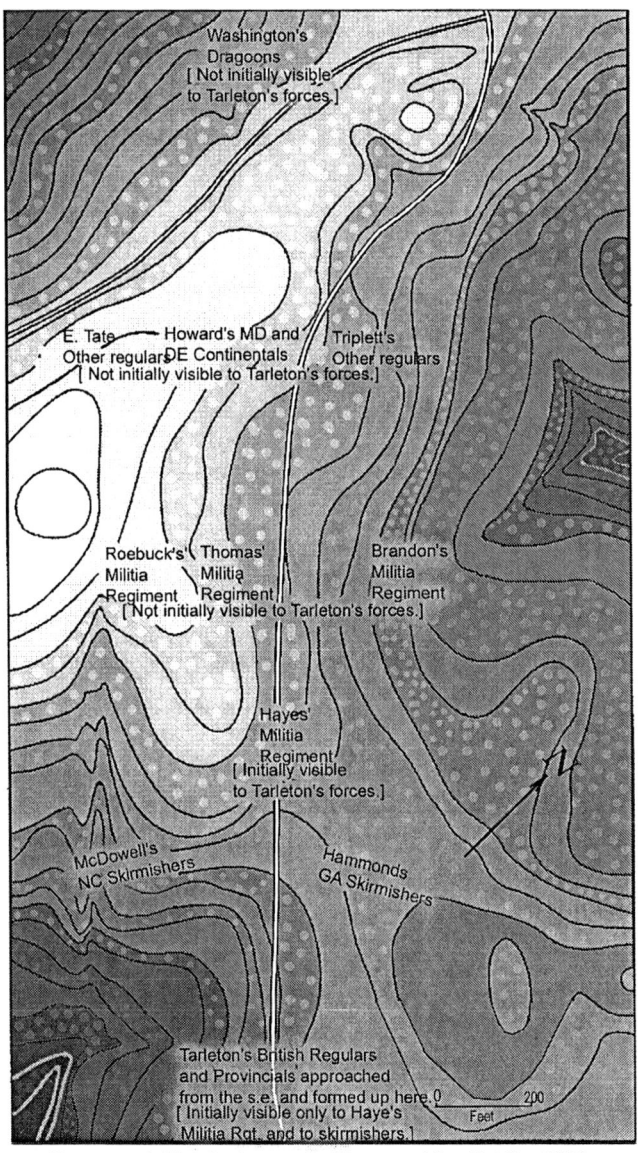

Cowpens: Initial deployment of forces. After Babits, 1998

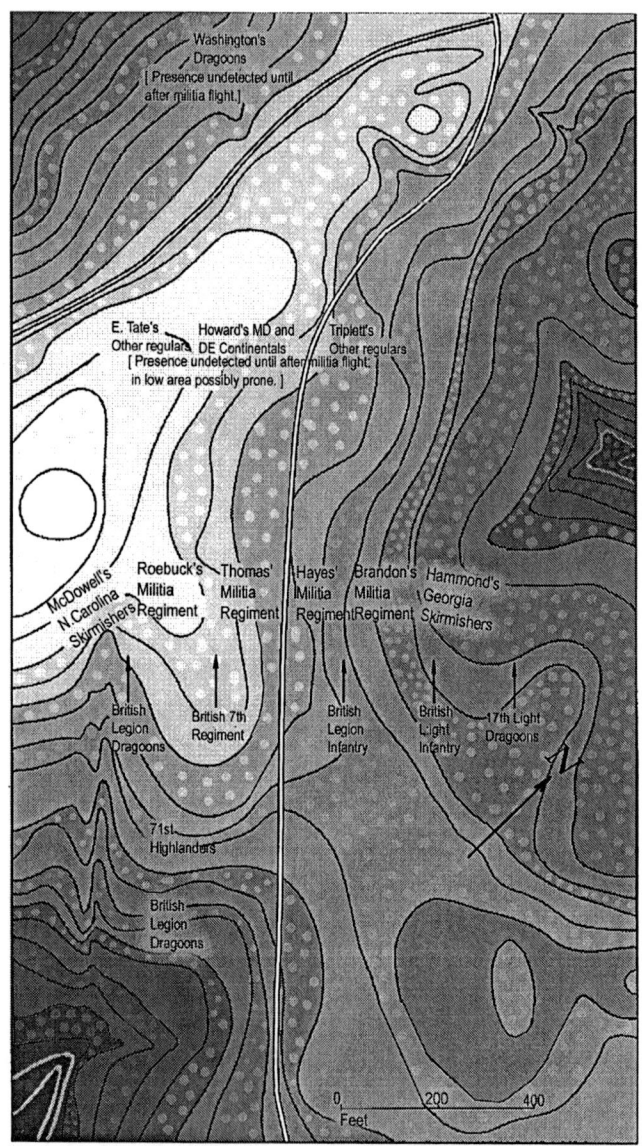

Cowpens: Tarleton's forces advance on militia line strengthened by skirmishers on the flanks. After Babits, 1998.

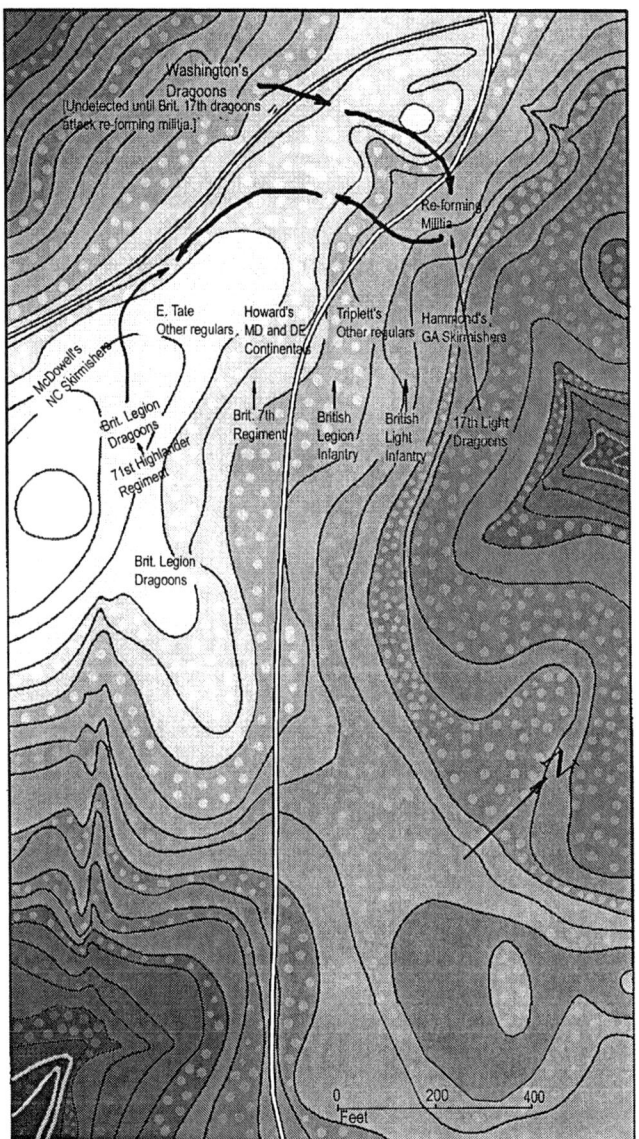

After costly encounter with militia line, Tarleton attempts simultaneous flanking movements with dragoons, both thwarted by Washington.
After Babits, 1998

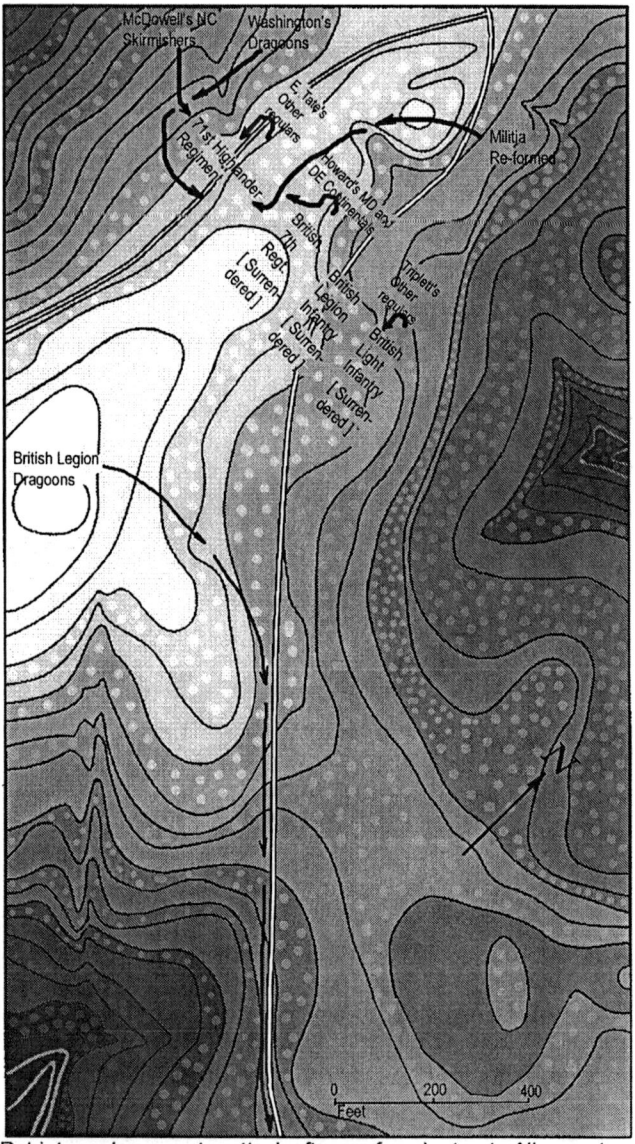

Patriot regulars counter-attack after confused retreat. All except 71st surrendered quickly. 71st is surrounded in "double envelopment". After Babits, 1998.

underestimated Morgan. Because the Flying Army was outnumbered two to one in infantry and three to one in cavalry, Morgan had called on the militia to join him at the cow pens. He had no choice but to depend on the militia, commanded by Col. Andrew Pickens, to help him stop Tarleton. Would it be another Camden?

Morgan posted his troops in three lines. The first, the skirmishers, were sharpshooters from North Carolina and Georgia. The second was a line of militia, who would be reinforced by the skirmishers when they fell back, commanded by Andrew Pickens. The third line was Continental Infantry commanded by Lt. Col. John Eager Howard. The cavalry, commanded by Lt. Col. William Washington, was posted in a swale behind the lines. The British would be lured into a series of killing zones (Babits, 1998).

At daybreak Tarleton's troops moved up the Green River Road. The morning was cold, wet and misty. Visibility was limited. Tarleton probably believed the Americans were rushing for the Broad River to escape into North Carolina. Seeing a single company, Hayes' Little River Militia, in the road ahead, Tarleton sent his dragoons forward to determine the enemy's strength and position. Rifle fire from the right and left side emptied saddles as the skirmishers, posted in the woods on either side of the road, fired.

Although Tarleton was Lord Cornwallis' most effective cavalry officer, he was no tactician. As the British had so often done before, Tarleton intended to clear the field of this militia with bayonets. He ordered his troops to attack. As the British line moved forward they were confronted with the second line which was now composed of several militia units and the skirmishers. Tarleton reported later that there were a thousand militia on the field (Tarleton, 1784) and recent research (Babits, 1998 ; Moss, 1991) support that claim. The militia line waited until the British were within killing range

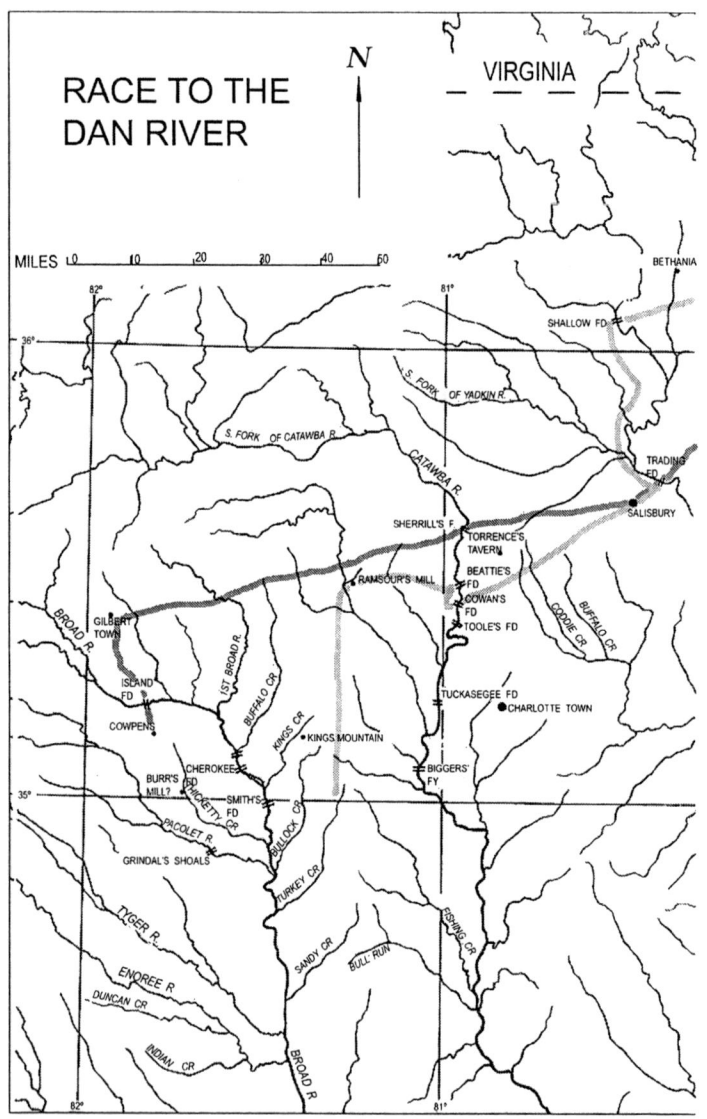

"Race to the Dan River" following Battle at the Cowpens. Darker gray shows approximate path of Morgan's/Greene's army. Lighter gray shows that of Cornwallis' army.

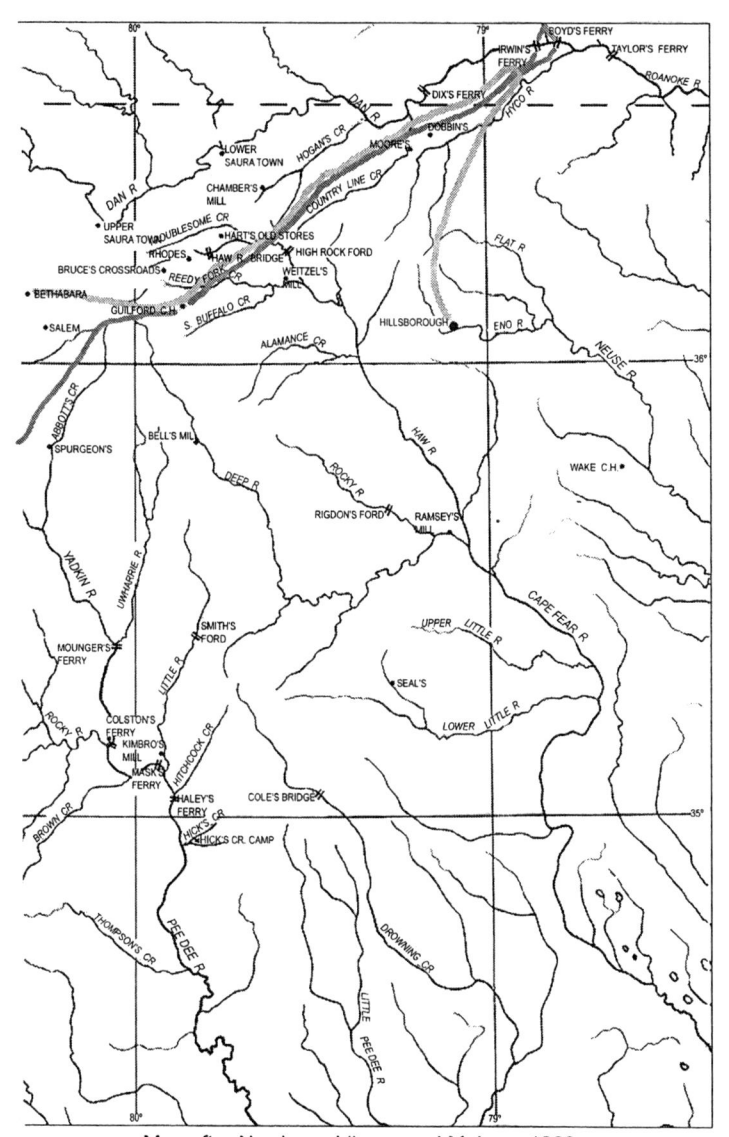

Map after Newberry Library and Malone, 1999.
Routes after "Another Such Victory", Baker, 1999.

before firing. It was aimed fire targeting officers and sergeants and the damage was considerable (McKenzie, 1786).

The militia line withdrew and the British line was now faced with the Continental Infantry. Even with the addition of reserves, the British line was overwhelmed by the combined force of the Continental line, Washington's mounted and the reformed militia. In less than an hour Tarleton had lost a fourth of Cornwallis' force, and all of the British light infantry in the south. Only Tarleton, his mounted officers, and some of his British Legion dragoons escaped.

Soon Cornwallis was in pursuit, determined to retrieve the 600 British soldiers Morgan held prisoner, and to destroy Morgan's army. When Greene heard of Morgan's victory at Cowpens, he moved to join Morgan and command the "Race to the Dan" (Buchanan, 1997). The Dan River was the border between North Carolina and Virginia and Virginia was the only area where the Americans could incarcerate such a large number of prisoners.

As the British trailed the Americans across river after river, Cornwallis, determined to lighten the load of his troops and move more rapidly, burned his baggage. It was an audacious move. However, when Cornwallis finally arrived at the Dan River, he found the Americans had crossed. The Continental Army was beyond the reach of the British, and the prisoners would be held at Fort Security near York, Pennsylvania for more than two years.

Lord Cornwallis had not only lost the prisoners, he had failed to destroy Daniel Morgan. He had failed to destroy General Greene's army, and in his campaign through North Carolina he had lost seventeen percent of his troops to disease, death or desertion (Konstam, 2002). Now Lord Cornwallis was over 200 miles from Camden (Buchanan, 1997), and without access to supplies and without baggage.

He may not have known before what the winter in North Carolina could be like, but he was learning now.

Major General Nathanael Greene was in Virginia where he could enlarge his army and procure supplies while Lord Cornwallis camped at Hillsboro, an inhospitable territory. He was without provisions for his sick and wounded. The British army dwindled while Greene's army increased.

When Greene was confident that his army was capable of taking the field, he moved to Guilford Courthouse, a site which he had surveyed on his trip north and had considered appropriate for battle. Here he would meet the attack of the British army. Morgan was no longer with the Continental Army since illness had forced him from the field, but Greene attempted to replicate Morgan's tactics which had won at Cowpens. There were differences. The lines at Guilford Courthouse were twice as far apart as the lines at Cowpens. The terrain was different in that wooded areas would obscure Greene's view as he attempted to command from the third line. Whereas Morgan had been able to survey and command his entire force at Cowpens, Greene would be hampered by his inability to monitor the action on the field.

On 15 March 1781 Cornwallis attacked with regular British troops and Hessians. He greatly outnumbered Greene in trained troops and he was contemptuous of the militia in Greene's first line. Although Greene was later critical of the performance of the militia, they had obeyed their orders. An officer of the 71st Highlanders recalled that half of his regiment dropped from militia fire.

The battle was fought in open fields, then in the woods where the British line had to break into smaller groups. As Continentals and British engaged, Cornwallis observed that his Guards were being hammered. Seeing the impasse and fearing that the momentum was favoring the Americans, Cornwallis ordered his artillery to fire into the line killing both American and British soldiers. As callous as it seems, it

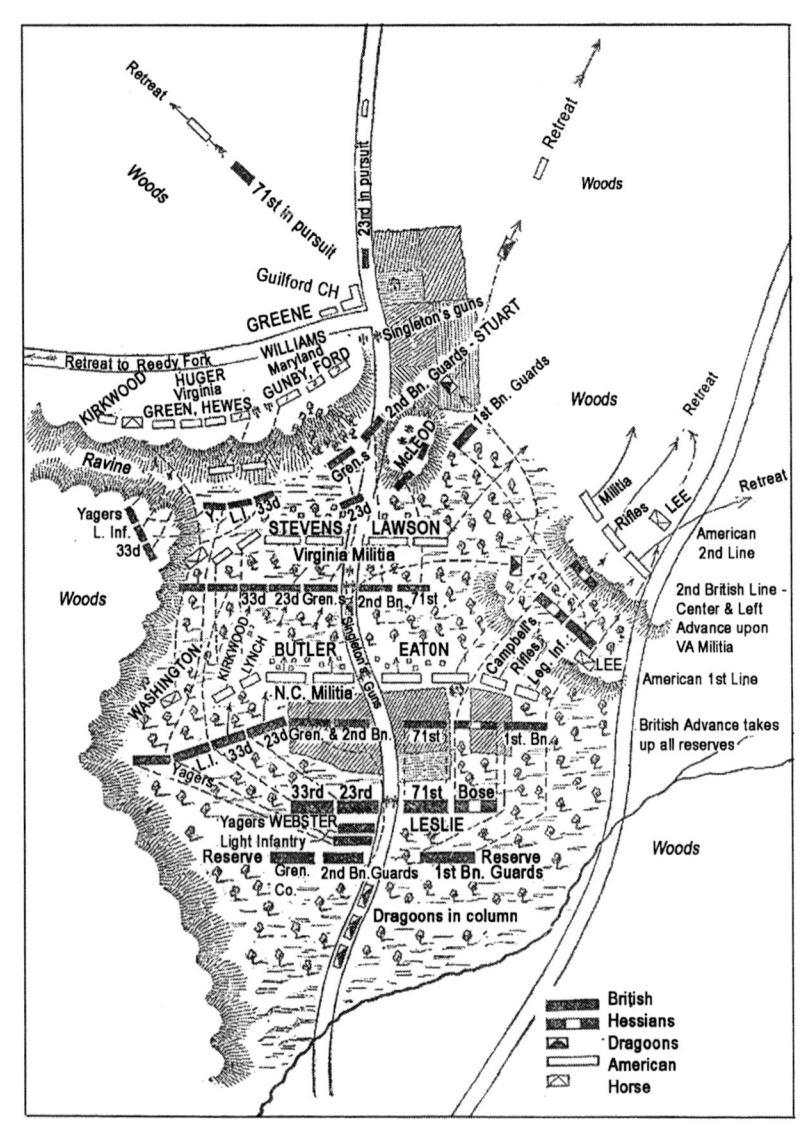

Battle at Guilford Courthouse
After H.B. Carrington, 1876

was successful and the Americans pulled back.

As the British pushed forward, part of the Continental line collapsed and Greene, fearful that he was being flanked, made the decision to retreat. He had the only army in the south and he did not intend to lose it. He moved from the field in good order and entrenched in a new position expecting Cornwallis to pursue (Baker, 1981).

Cornwallis had won a pyrrhic victory. He had won the battle, he had kept the field, but he had lost 27% of his troops (Baker, 1981). Twenty-nine of the British officers were killed or wounded and, stranded in the middle of North Carolina in the bitterness of the late winter, the British Army could not afford to lose such experienced leaders (Baker, 1981).

When word of the victory reached England, Charles James Fox, a politician in opposition to the King's government, addressed the House of Commons, "Another such victory would ruin the British Army" (Baker, 1981).

Now, with a poorly clad army, large numbers of wounded and a horde of camp followers, Lord Cornwallis had outrun his supplies in a hostile, unforgiving territory. He was left to ponder his options. One possibility was to return to South Carolina but to retreat would appear as a defeat and it was not in Cornwallis' nature to abandon his plan to move north. The other was to move toward the nearest port, Wilmington, North Carolina, where he could rest his exhausted troops, tend to his wounded, and re-supply his army.

Cornwallis chose Wilmington, and after the troops were recuperated, would again start for Virginia. He would campaign in the interior of that colony until an exasperated Clinton ordered him to establish an anchorage on the Chesapeake where he could be re-supplied. Point Comfort (Hampton, Virginia) was Clinton's choice but, always defiant, Cornwallis rejected that site as unsuitable. He would choose Yorktown.

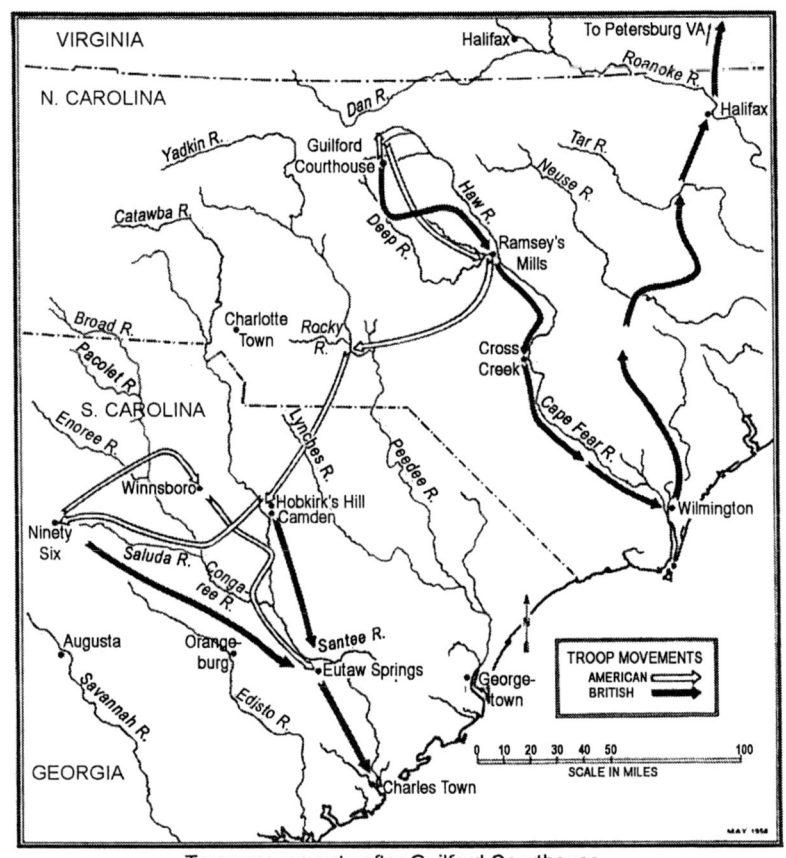

Troop movements after Guilford Courthouse
After National Park Service (1958)

CHAPTER III

GREENE'S DECISION

As Lord Cornwallis moved his suffering army away from Guilford Courthouse and toward relief at Wilmington, Major General Nathanael Greene followed to Ramsay's Mill. He, too, was pondering his options. Meanwhile, Greene ordered his cavalry to follow the British army and take stragglers prisoner. This action also gave Cornwallis the impression that Greene's entire army was in pursuit.

Although Cornwallis claimed victory at Guilford Court House, and Greene had missed an opportunity to win a decisive victory, the morale of the Continental troops was high (Lee, 1812). Although the militia had not regrouped as Greene had hoped, (given the success which the militia had given Morgan at Cowpens), most of the more experienced Continentals had fought bravely (Lee, 1812). Lt. Col. William Washington's cavalry had engaged the feared Guards, and prompted Cornwallis' desperate artillery fire into that line, killing many of his own men. Greene was confident that, if Congress would forward him men and supplies, he could defeat the British Army (F. V. Greene, 1893). Time was on Greene's side. Cornwallis could not continue to absorb the numbers of casualties he had taken at King's Mountain, Cowpens and Guilford Courthouse.

Leaving the American wounded with local Quakers, Greene considered his future campaign. A momentous responsibility for the entire embattled south rested on his shoulders.

His strategy in the south had been to inflict as much damage on the British forces as possible and he had been successful. Morgan at Cowpens had destroyed one quarter of Cornwallis's army. At Guilford Courthouse, Cornwallis lost another twenty-seven percent of his force killed or wounded. It was Greene's policy to meet the enemy when and where he chose. With Lord Cornwallis moving to the coast, it was time for Greene to refine his strategy. What did Lord Cornwallis intend to do? Would he rest his army and then return to solidify his control of South Carolina? Or would he turn his attention to Virginia? Greene had no way of knowing but he had to be ready for any eventuality.

As Greene rested his army he was himself recovering from fatigue. It was reported that he had not taken off his clothes since leaving Hick's Creek to join Morgan (V. F. Greene, 1893). Rarely did he enjoy more than four hours of sleep at night and often, not that. As the army rested General Greene would develop a new strategy. As usual, he was receptive to opinions of his officers (Lee, 1812), but the decision would be his alone. Perhaps at no time in the Southern Campaign did Greene's superior mind have more impact on the outcome of the war. He considered all the possibilities (Lee, 1812).

Although not knowing what Lord Cornwallis might do after he had re-supplied his army at Wilmington, General Greene decided against following the British army to engage it closer to the coast. To move his army into an area close to British ports would be disastrous. He decided to move towards South Carolina.

There were excellent reasons for the choice. Strong militia leaders like Francis Marion, Thomas Sumter, and

Andrew Pickens had demonstrated that they could operate in the state which was British occupied but not conquered. Although still dissatisfied with the militia conduct at Guilford Courthouse, Greene knew that he could depend on their assistance.

If Lord Cornwallis should decide to return to South Carolina, Greene could move westward toward the upcountry militia. This militia had turned out in great numbers to fight and defeat Tarleton at Cowpens. Finally, if there was a need to move northward toward Washington's army, he could move through Charlotte and the Yadkin River Valley. Greene was familiar with this area since he had recently traversed it with Morgan's Flying Army on their route to move the prisoners from the Battle of Cowpens to Virginia. Certainly, if he were pressed in that area, he could rely on the Over Mountain Men of Shelby and Sevier who had performed heroically at King's Mountain.

However, Greene was not only a student of military history, but was an astute observer of political history. Although the French had a treaty with the Americans which prevented making peace with Great Britain unilaterally, Greene was aware that the French had lost some of their enthusiasm for the cause of American independence after the disastrous defeat of the Continental Army at the Battle of Camden in August, 1780. Also, recent British casualties might force England to consider making peace with France without consideration of the American interests. If hostilities ceased, Great Britain would expect to retain the territory which it held. This was the principle of international law, **uti possidetis,**, practiced at that time and even today.

The British had been pushed out of Boston and Philadelphia, but held ports along the Atlantic seaboard. However, the only colonies they occupied totally were South Carolina and Georgia. After the recent victory at Guilford Courthouse they would claim territory in North Carolina.

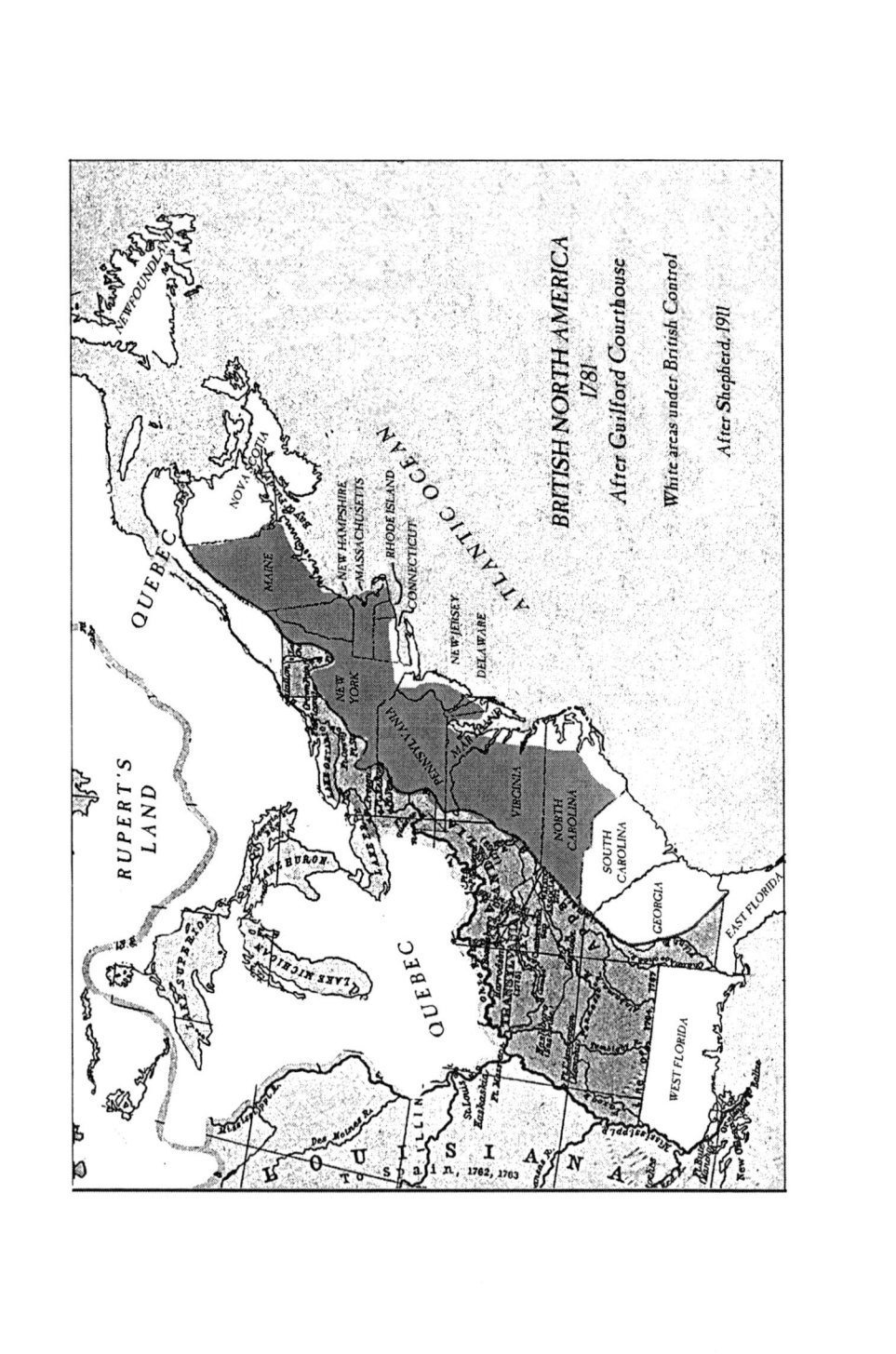

BRITISH NORTH AMERICA
1781-
After Guilford Courthouse

White areas under British Control

After Shepherd, 1911

England might be willing to settle for that rich, productive area. Greene saw the threat. Believing that the Americans could win given time, it was still imperative to take back the occupied territories before the situation became a matter of deliberation by France and Great Britain, with or without American participation.

Greene's new goal was to retrieve territory, and his strategy was determined here. He would attack the British stronghold of Camden while patriot militia attacked smaller posts in the area simultaneously. This concurrent action would prevent the British commander, Lord Rawdon, from moving detachments posted at Fort Motte or Fort Watson to bolster his defenses at Camden. Lt. Col. Henry Lee (Light Horse Harry) would move again into the swamps of the Pee Dee and Santee Rivers and campaign with militia leader Brigadier General Francis Marion. The two had combined their forces before Lee had been recalled to join Greene at Guilford Courthouse and the combination had been productive (Lee, 1812). Now they would attack posts and control the communication lines between the British headquarters at Charleston and the outposts at Camden and Ninety-Six (Lee, 1812).

The decision was made. While Lord Cornwallis would turn to the north in a campaign that ended at Yorktown, General Greene would move south and challenge the British occupation of South Carolina and Georgia, a campaign which would lead to Eutaw Springs.

Decision made, no time was lost. Greene sent word of his intentions to Pickens and Sumter instructing them to start mustering their militia. On 6 April 1781 Greene dispatched Lee's Legion with orders to join Francis Marion, now called the Swamp Fox, in the swamps in eastern Carolina and to apprise him of the new strategy.

On 14 April Lee joined forces with Marion who had just completed a month-long campaign against Col. John Watson

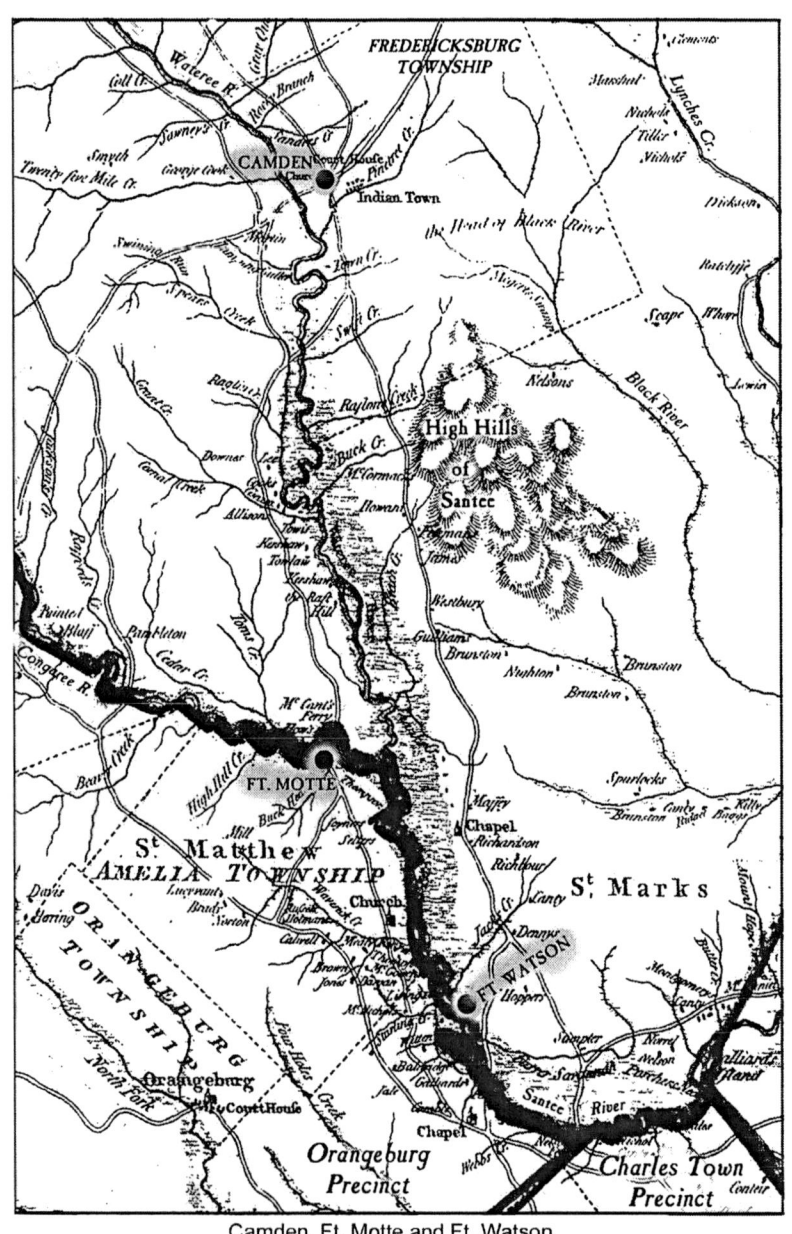

Camden, Ft. Motte and Ft. Watson
Mouson, 1775, with forts added and with minor editing for legibility

and his detachment of 64th Regiment of Foot. The engagements along the Black, Santee and Sampit Rivers had inflicted heavy casualties on Watson's force, but left Marion's men without powder or shot (James, 1821). However, Lee and Marion moved quickly towards Fort Watson, a British post on Scott's Lake, which guarded a supply route from Charleston to Camden.

On the evening of 15 April Lee and Marion sieged the fort. The stockade was built on an Indian mound and the area around it had been cleared so that the approach to the fort allowed no protection for the attackers (Lee, 1812). The fort was well fortified, the detachment of the 64th Regiment of Foot was well supplied with arms, food and water. Without a field piece Lee and Marion were unable to take the stockade until Major Maham of Marion's Brigade suggested constructing a tower from which riflemen could fire into the stockade (Lee, 1812; James, 1821). Working parties were dispatched to collect axes, to cut, to carry and to construct. On the morning of 23 April the tower was complete and the British commander, Lt. McKay, unable to escape the rifle fire from the men protected on a platform on top of the tower, surrendered the fort (Lee, 1812). "By taking it Gen. Marion obtained supplies of ammunition, which he soon turned to good advantage." (James 1821:110) The prisoners were moved toward General Greene's army north of Camden.

Meanwhile, General Greene had moved his troops toward Camden arriving in the area on 19 April. Word of Fort Watson's capture and the prisoners taken there reached him on 24 April as he was encamped on a ridge beyond Camden, called Hobkirk's Hill. On the morning of 25 April the British commander at Camden, Lord Rawdon, moved his troops against Greene's force. In a hotly contested battle, Lord Rawdon was the victor. General Greene withdrew from the field towards Sanders Creek. Pursued by British cavalry

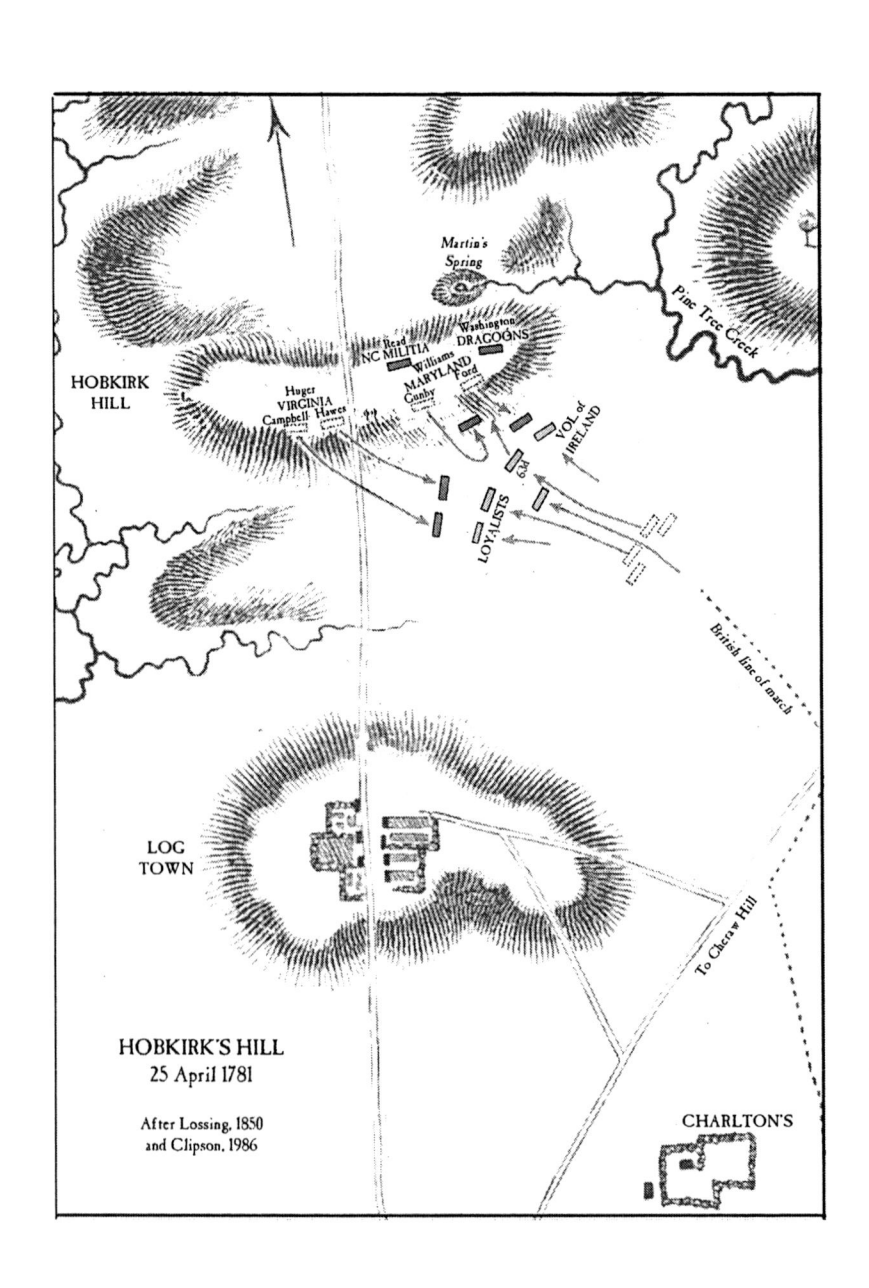

HOBKIRK'S HILL
25 April 1781

After Lossing, 1850
and Clipson, 1986

under the command of Major James Coffin, Lt. Col. William Washington executed an ambush which resulted in several British dragoons killed or taken prisoner. The rest fled although Major Coffin tried to regroup before he left the field.

Although the losses on both sides were about equal (Lee, 1812), the British clearly won the engagement and Lord Rawdon attempted to follow this win with the total destruction of Greene's army. However, learning that Marion and Lee were to his rear, Lord Rawdon withdrew to the safety of his fortifications at Camden.

General Greene, disappointed that General Sumter had not joined him as ordered (Lee, 1812), and depressed by his loss, soon realized that Lord Rawdon had achieved little by the British victory. Camden was isolated and needed relief. Lord Rawdon had many sick and wounded soldiers and meager supplies. Lee and Marion now controlled the supply lines and Rawdon lacked the force to reestablish them. The supplies which had been intended for Camden were at Fort Motte and that post was under siege by Marion and Lee. Rawdon decided to give up Camden and all the territory north of the Congaree River (Lee, 1812). He sent orders for Ninety-Six and Fort Granby to be evacuated and to strengthen Orangeburg. However, Greene's plans to control communications had been successful. None of Rawdon's messages reached their destination (Lee, 1812).

On 10 May 1781 Camden was evacuated and Lord Rawdon moved his troops, local Tories, and their slaves down the King's Highway towards Nelson's Ferry. Lee reports:

> Previous to his lordship's departure he burned the jail, the mills, and some private houses, and destroyed all the stores which he could not take with him. He carried off four

or five hundred negroes, and all the most obnoxious loyalists accompanied him. (Lee, 1812:345).

Greene correctly guessed that Rawdon would attempt to relieve Fort Motte to recover his supplies. Fort Motte was a fortified mansion on a hill commanding the confluence of the Wateree and Congaree Rivers. The British commander, Lt. McPherson, had no artillery and the patriot forces had one unmounted six-pounder sent by Greene after the battle at Hobkirk's Hill. An offer to surrender had been refused and a siege continued. Now, with Lord Rawdon's retreating troops moving toward Fort Motte, a sense of urgency prevailed. Waiting until the sun had dried the shingles on the mansion's roof, brimstone and rosin (James, 1821) were used to set the roof on fire. When the British soldiers went on the roof to tear off the blazing shingles, they were raked with rifle fire and cannister shot. Lt. McPherson surrendered the fort, and the supplies which were intended for Camden now supplied the American forces.

Shortly after the fall of Fort Motte, General Greene arrived at the scene. This was his first meeting with Brigadier General Francis Marion although he was well-acquainted with the "Swamp Fox" by reputation and achievements.

Marion had been despondent. He had spent the fall and winter campaigning in the Santee, Pee Dee and Black River swamps. The British had sent five commanders into those swamps to kill him and had failed. Marion's Brigade had embarrassed the British and intimidated their Tory supporters, but Marion was tired. His militia often did not muster in great enough numbers to satisfy him. He was always without sufficient powder and shot. He considered resigning and traveling to Philadelphia and offering his services there. Although a militia brigadier general, Marion

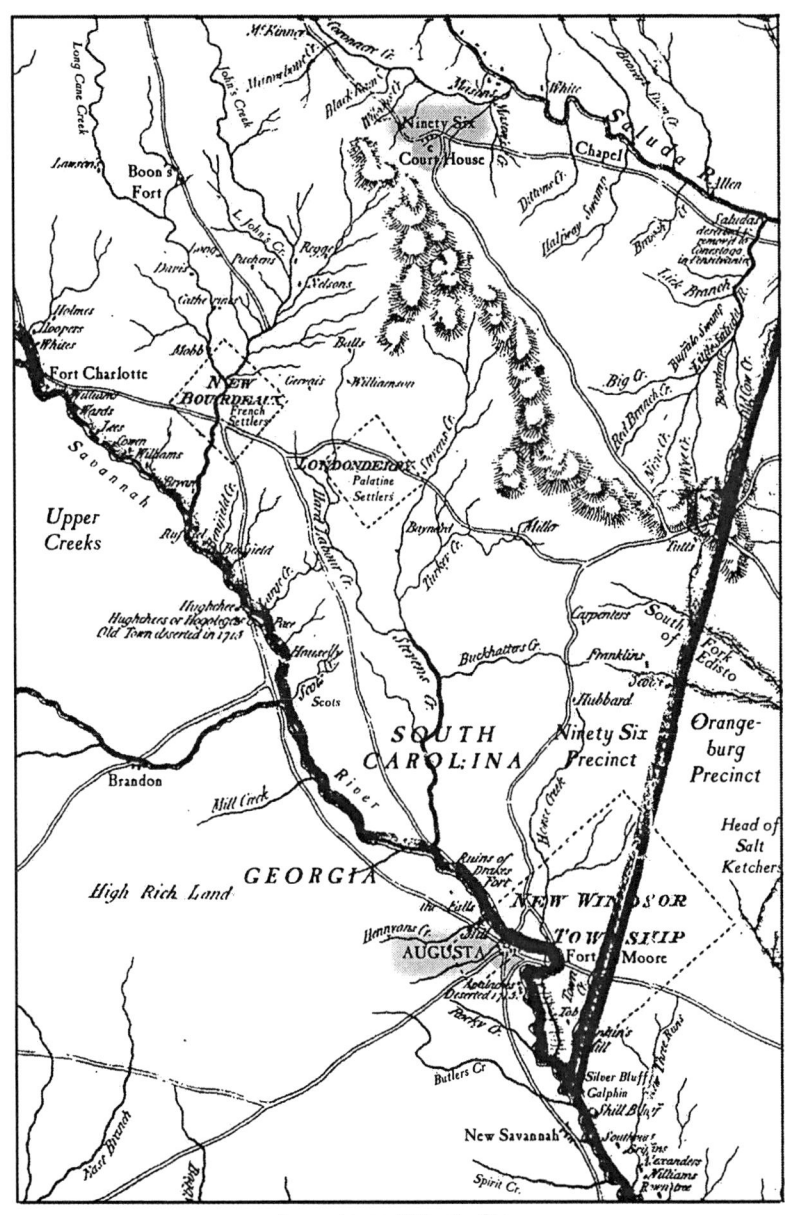

Augusta and Ninety Six
Mouzon, 1775, with minor text editing for legibility.

also held a commission as a lieutenant colonel in the Continental Army. Perhaps Marion was responsive to the orders of his commanding general, or saw the wisdom and possibilities of the strategy but, for whatever reason, Marion left the meeting with renewed vigor and moved his militia towards the British garrison at Georgetown. There was no more talk of resignation.

Lt. Col. Lee was ordered to Fort Granby. Militia commander, Brigadier General Thomas Sumter was campaigning in the Orangeburg area and had captured that British outpost.

Lord Rawdon, who was encamped at Monck's Corner, saw his area of occupation dwindle as Fort Granby, Orangeburg, and Georgetown were taken by the patriot forces. Lee observes that one month after Greene had moved toward Camden, the territory north of the Santee and Congaree Rivers had been retaken as well as some posts to the south. Now, only Ninety-Six remained as a major stronghold beyond the ports of Savannah and Charleston (Lee, 1812).

Continuing his strategy of concurrent attacks, Greene ordered Pickens and Lee to the Augusta area, to neutralize that British held area. There they were joined by Georgia militia, the Georgia Refugees, commanded by Lt. Col. Elijah Clarke. The attacks on the forts protecting Augusta, Fort Grierson and Fort Cornwallis, were successful and 5 June 1781 Augusta was in the hands of the Americans.

At the same time the British at Georgetown were under increasing pressure from Marion's forces. The British evacuated that port on 6 June 1781 (Lumpkin 1981).

On 22 May 1871 General Nathanael Greene had invested the Star Fort at Ninety-Six, the last British stronghold in the interior. Lt. Col. Cruger, a Loyalist from New York, and an officer in a unit of provincial regulars, commanded the post. The Star Fort was heavily fortified and manned by provincial regulars of New York and New Jersey in addition to other Loyalist troops. These soldiers had served in South Carolina since the beginning of the Southern Campaign and had seen considerable action in the northern states prior to that. The Loyalist troops were local militia from the Ninety-Six district.

The configuration of the Star Fort made a direct attack impossible so Greene had started digging siege lines. Greene was always mindful of where Lord Cornwallis was campaigning and where Lord Rawdon was situated. A message from Cornwallis to Rawdon had been intercepted and the news was distressing. Replacements were due to arrive in Charleston and Cornwallis ordered Rawdon to prevent those fresh troops from debarking and to send them immediately to Virginia. With Rawdon unaware of those orders, Greene suspected that these troops would provide Rawdon with the manpower he needed to move against Greene at Ninety-Six and to relieve the garrison.

Greene was correct. When 2000 troops from Ireland arrived in Charleston Rawdon commandeered the flank companies of those replacements and, along with his own unit, the Volunteers of Ireland, and South Carolina Royalist commanded by John Coffin, started for Ninety-Six.

The Americans had interrupted the communications between Cornwallis and Rawdon, and Greene had excellent intelligence of his own. He knew of Rawdon's plan and ordered militia general Thomas Sumter to move in front of Rawdon's advance and impede the British progress. Sumter either would not or could not follow those orders (Lee, 1812), and Rawdon arrived at Ninety-Six on 21 June 1781. Now outnumbered, Greene made the decision that would save his army, and withdrew towards the north. The siege had cost him 57 dead and 70 wounded (Lumpkin, 1981). The Americans had inflicted 85 casualties on the enemy, 27 killed and 58 wounded (Lumpkin, 1981).

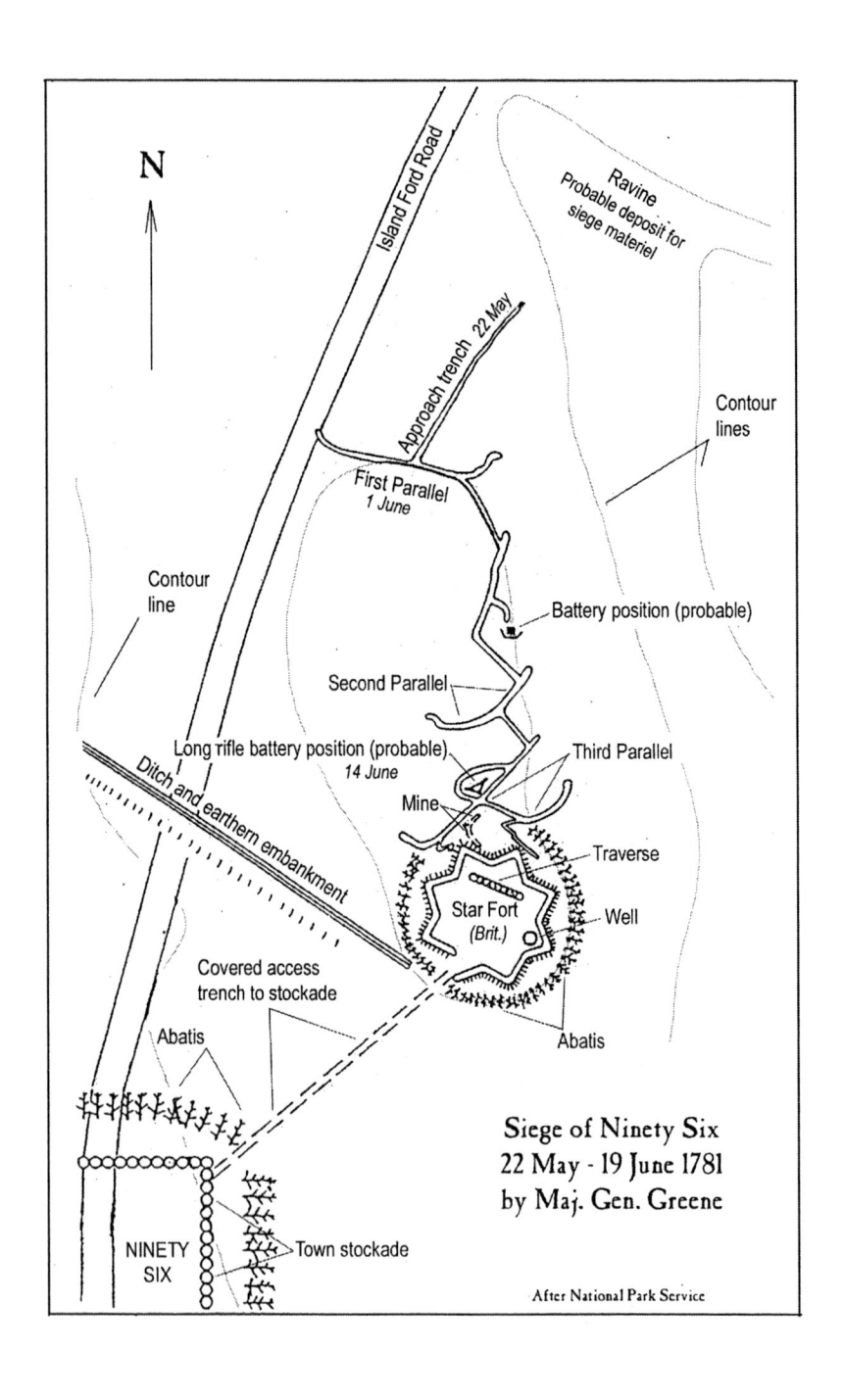

Siege of Ninety Six
22 May - 19 June 1781
by Maj. Gen. Greene

After National Park Service

Rawdon relieved the fort and ordered Col. Cruger to evacuate the troops and to offer safe conduct to Charleston to any Tories who wished to accompany them. Then Cruger was to join Rawdon in his pursuit of Greene.

The two armies maneuvered in the Orangeburg area but Greene was careful not to be caught between Rawdon's force and the retreating British from the garrison at Ninety-Six. Although Rawdon's army outnumbered the Americans, he hesitated to attack. Certainly a more aggressive commander would have made the attempt but Rawdon was ill. He had suffered a series of debilitating diseases since arriving in South Carolina and wished to return to the British Isles to recuperate. He was not the only one who was suffering. The newly arrived troops from Ireland who, in their woolen uniforms, had been rapidly marched to Ninety-Six, had also suffered from South Carolina's brutal summer and fifty died of heat stroke.

Lord Rawdon turned over the command of his troops to Lt. Col. Alexander Stewart, an officer who had recently arrived from Ireland. Rawdon returned to Charleston with about 500 men. While waiting passage for New York he concurred with Lt. Col. Nesbit Balfour, the commander in Charleston, in an event which had serious consequences.

Major Frazer of the South Carolina Royalists had captured the patriot Isaac Hayne, a colonel in the South Carolina militia, and turned him over to the British commander in Charleston. Hayne was tried and hanged. The justice of this has long been debated and Rawdon defended the decision in later years. (Rawdon letter to Lee in Lee, 1812). The Americans thought the punishment unjust and Francis Marion, the militia general who had commissioned Hayne and his officers, was enraged.

The spring had been unusually wet and the summer heat and high humidity made soldiers of both armies miserable. British supplies were low but the American troops were subsisting on rice and frogs and an occasional alligator (Lee, 1812). Greene needed forage for his many horses, food for his men and rest and treatment for his wounded. He crossed the Congaree and Wateree rivers and established a camp at the High Hills of the Santee, high ground beyond the Wateree. Here he would establish a camp of ease and would train his troops and attempt to accumulate more support for his army.

Lt. Col. Stewart moved his troops to the south of the Congaree close to where Fort Motte had stood, on property owned by a patriot family, the Thomsons. Here he could see the campfires of Greene's camp but the enemies were divided by a large body of water which had accumulated in the flood plains of the Wateree and Congaree.

Greene ordered Lee and Washington to patrol the area and move as many supplies as possible out of reach of the British while the remainder of his army encamped in the relative comfort of the High Hills. Now the two armies watched and waited just a few miles from Eutaw Springs.

CHAPTER IV

AT THE HIGH HILLS

Since Major General Nathanael Greene had made the decision to move into the south and to challenge the British occupation of South Carolina and Georgia, his infantry had marched about 1000 miles. The previous winter and the spring had been unusually wet, and now the scorching heat and the high humidity of the Carolina summer had presented almost intolerable hardships on Greene's weary army. Half of the troops were ill (Lee, 1812), and food was in short supply. Lee reports that the rice, which was served instead of bread, was acceptable to the men of the deep south but was unpalatable to those of Maryland and Delaware who preferred wheat.

Not only was food in short supply, but clothing and weapons were not being supplied as had been promised. Although 2000 troops had been promised from Virginia they were not forthcoming, much to Greene's great regret. With British troops in Virginia, that colony had lost its enthusiasm for supplying men or supplies to Greene's army. In spite of the grim situation, Greene continued to drill his available troops in the camp in the High Hills of the Santee.

The High Hills of the Santee lie along the north bank of the Wateree River on the Charleston to Camden road.

Raised above the flood plain of the Wateree, the elevation provided some relief from the oppressive heat. Early settlers sought such spots as a relief from the summer heat and the malaria which seemed to accompany it. Not knowing that mosquitoes spread the disease, the planters were aware that higher elevations in the sand hills were healthier for their families. Now Nathanael Greene hoped that the healing hills would restore the health of his suffering army.

The greatest threat to the men as they drilled and drilled was disease, and the most dreaded among those was smallpox. The disease had been widespread in the Old World for centuries and had long been known to be contagious and very often fatal. The patients were racked with fever and covered with a rash which turned to deep pustules and left the body pitted with scars. Lord Rawdon was reported to have survived smallpox but was left with an ugly pitted face.

The smallpox was brought to the New World with first the explorers and then the early settlers. The unprotected native populations were highly susceptible and many tribes were almost annihilated.

Although inoculation with a live virus had been tried in Europe and Africa with some success, it was slow to become practice on this continent. Although a few physicians were aware of its potential, there was widespread opposition due to fear and ignorance. However, after several outbreaks in Boston, an attempt at mass inoculations was made. Yet the process was cumbersome as the inoculated patient would have a milder case of the disease but that could still be spread to others as a more virulent form so quarantines were required. In the 1740's an epidemic in Charleston prompted an attempt to inoculate but the South Carolina Assembly prohibited it (Reiss, 1998).

Although George Washington had authorized some inoculations of Continental soldiers, it was not universal and, it can be supposed, that few of the Continental soldiers accompanying Greene at this time were protected against smallpox.

The composition of an army and the close confines of camp life contributed to contagion. Since smallpox was highly contagious and rural settlers were rarely immune or inoculated, the assembly of new, rural settlers into the army spread the disease. The recruitment of the North Carolina units had been delayed because of an outbreak of smallpox, and the Georgia Refugees had been disbanded for a time after being ravaged with the disease evidently contracted during their service at Augusta.

Nor was smallpox the only debilitating disease the army had to confront. There were diseases spread by insects such as mosquitoes and lice but those means of spreading the diseases were not understood at that time. Malaria, spread by mosquitoes, was wide-spread in the south and few were immune to it. In the summer heat insects flourished and malaria was common. Although it was not as deadly as smallpox, Lord Rawdon suffered from it frequently enough to have his health so impaired that he returned to England to recover. The aches and fever of the disease incapacitated the sufferer.

The settlers at the time referred to the air in the swamp as miasmic and believed that the vapor which resulted when the dampness rotted the vegetation was poisonous and caused malaria. Although this was not true, the movement away from the swamps in the humid weather did remove them from the mosquitoes and reduced the chances of malaria.

Another mosquito-born illness was yellow fever and it too caused the infected much pain and suffering. Its name came from the jaundiced appearance of the skin. Lt. Col. Banastre Tarleton was so afflicted that he was not able to command his troops and possibly missed an opportunity to save Major Patrick Ferguson at King's Mountain. Typhus was spread by lice and the crowded conditions of camp life made the soldier susceptible. Wars exacerbated the situation and many died.

With such large numbers of men in close proximity, inadequate sewage disposal and tainted water presented opportunities for typhoid fever and dysentery. Both, although not often fatal, could, with complications, kill.

Dysentery (camp fever) was especially debilitating for prolonged diarrhea could dehydrate and kill the sufferer.

Flu and pneumonia were illnesses expected among troops. The flu was likely to be incapacitating but pneumonia, before the advent of penicillin, was often fatal.

Exertion in the summer heat caused heat strokes and heat exhaustion. Before the Battle of Monmouth Courthouse, New Jersey, Hessians rapidly marching in their heavy uniforms suffered from the June heat and fifty-nine died of heat exhaustion (Reiss, 1998). Lord Rawdon's dash to break the siege at Ninety-Six had resulted in the death of fifty soldiers of the flank companies which had recently arrived in Charleston after having been posted in much more temperate Ireland.

There is evidence that Greene was aware of the dangers of heat stroke and exhaustion and drilled his men in the cooler mornings and evenings, and avoided the mid-day heat as much as possible. The possibility, however, for heat-related casualties existed during the exertions of battle.

The treatments for fevers and intestinal ailments (bleeding, purging and blistering), caused the patients great discomfort and often exacerbated the problem.

In addition to the diseases and injuries the soldiers were prone to, General Greene's encampment had to deal with the wounded which were hospitalized there. Without a means to combat infections, many died of wounds which would be considered minor today. To ward off the possibility of infections, limbs which were badly injured were amputated.

Without anesthetics or antibiotics the incidents of suffering and death were excessive.

The many hazards of soldiering in that time, and the hardships endured by these Patriots and their Loyalist enemies, make the sacrifices they made monumental.

Greene's army was not alone in its suffering. Lt. Col. Lee and Lt. Col. Washington patrolled the area with their mounted troops, gathering intelligence, moving provisions out of reach of the British army and intercepting British reconnaissance parties. They killed or captured scouts for the British and from prisoners learned that the British army, now camped at Col. Thomson's plantation just below Fort Motte, also suffered from heat and disease.

Although the two armies were fewer than 20 miles apart, they were separated by the flood plains at the confluence of the Congaree and Wateree Rivers, where the two join to form the Santee River. Due to the extremely wet winter, the bottom lands were flooded, forming a huge lake which divided and protected the armies from attack. However, the flood waters were the breeding grounds of a variety of insects, many transmitting disease to the sweltering troops.

Although the Continental army was encamped at the High Hills, there were units in the field putting pressure on the British outposts. Militia General Thomas Sumter was conducting what is known as the Dog Days Campaign. With Lt. Col. Lee and General Francis Marion, Sumter moved into the low country to deprive the British of supplies and safe havens. At the Battle of Quimby Bridge the patriot troops attacked entrenched British troops. Although Marion and Lee were dissatisfied with Sumter's command in that they suffered extensive casualties, the British withdrew toward Charleston after the battle.

In spite of the difficulties of the encampment at the High Hills, Greene continued an extensive correspondence with members of Congress, with General Washington, and

LaFayette, as well as his units in South Carolina. In late July there was considerable anxiety when it was learned that Lord Cornwallis' troops were aboard ship in Hampton Roads, Virginia. There was no intelligence as to where they were headed. If New York, that would put additional pressure on Washington's army which had been able to function without pressure from Clinton. Clinton had gone into a defensive mode after leaving part of his army with Lord Cornwallis. Or would Cornwallis return to Charleston to reestablish British control in the Carolinas?

There was considerable relief when it was learned that Cornwallis had landed at Yorktown on the York River in Virginia. This site had a deep water harbor where the British Navy could operate. However, the movement of British troops in Virginia had repercussions in South Carolina. Virginia had promised to send Greene two thousand militia but due to the British threat in that state, those troops were never sent.

There were further disappointments. Greene had ordered Cols. Shelby and Sevier to muster their Over Mountain militia and join him at the High Hills, but Indian attacks on the frontier made it necessary for them to stay to protect that area. Greene also expected about one hundred and fifty Georgia Refugees (militia) to join him but smallpox had so depleted their ranks that they were unable to respond.

There was some good news. Francis Marion had forced the British from Georgetown and was now on the lower Santee. The patriots moved supplies away from the river where small British vessels were searching for supplies for Charleston in that area rich in rice. Marion's campaigning kept the British from attempting to move to Winyah Bay and Georgetown.

After Col. Isaac Hayne had been hanged in Charleston, General Greene had warned Francis Marion not to attempt retaliation at that time. However, on 18 August 1781 Marion suggested that he could take 200 men to the aid of the patriot militia close to Charleston.

On 20 August Greene concurred. (Greene's Papers, 1997). Traveling at night to avoid detection, Marion moved to the Edisto River and prepared an ambush for Major Fraser and his troops at Parker's Ferry. Major Fraser had been the British commander who had captured Isaac Hayne. Although reports of this encounter are available in James (1821) and in Greene's Papers (1997) there was little certainty about the casualties inflicted since Marion withdrew his men after the initial ambush.

A more complete account was written by a participant in the action who fought for the British.

> We proceeded as far as the Combahee (South Carolina) River. This was a foraging party to procure rice, etc., for the hospitals, and after completing the object intended we commenced our march back and we halted at Colonel Haines' Plantation the night after he was brought home and buried in his garden. I saw his grave. In the afternoon of the next day we left his plantation, and as we had got intelligence that General Marion was collecting a body of Troops to give us annoyance on our route, the order of march was changed, the Infantry and Artillery in front, and the Cavalry in the lead. We marched in this order until we came to a long swamp, a mile or so from Parker's Ferry, when we heard a few shots in front, and Major Fraser ordered the Cavalry to advance, seeing some Troops at a long distance off, and supposing them to be the enemy, charged over this long causeway and fell into an

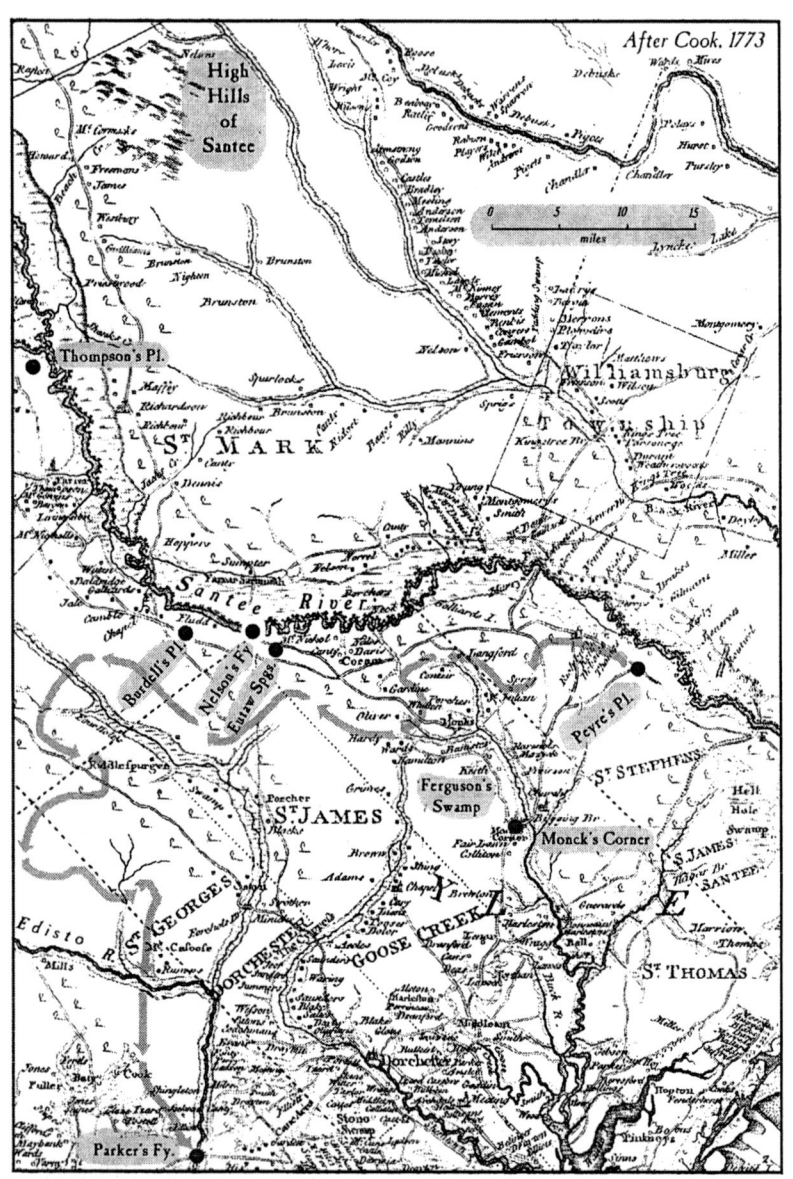

Marion's precise route from Peyre's plantation to Parker's Ferry is not known, but one such as shown would have taken him the 100 miles he is believed to have taken, riding at night, to reach the Edisto without it being known he had left Peyre's.

ambuscade, laid by the enemy, and we received the most galling fire ever Troops experienced. We saw only the flash of the pieces the enemy was so complete hid from our view, and we had only to push forward men and horses falling before and behind. We lost one hundred twenty-five killed and a great many wounded, and the enemy retired without the loss of a man. All our Artillery were killed or wounded before they could bring their guns to bear upon the enemy–we halted at Parker's Ferry that night, dropped our wounded, and the next morning collected our dead and buried them, and then proceeded on our route until we reached Dorchester without any molestation from the enemy.
(Jarvis, nd: 727-728)

American accounts indicate far fewer British dead than the Jarvis account. Jarvis was unaware of any patriot casualties but Marion reported that he had one private killed and two privates wounded.

Marion returned to the Santee area to learn that he had been ordered to join General Greene who was now ready to move against the British force.

When the decision was made to move against Lt. Col. Stewart, Major General Nathanael Greene had two options as to a route for his army. He could move downstream along the north bank of the Santee River and attempt to cross at Nelson's Ferry or in that vicinity. However, the wet spring and summer rains, which had deluged the flood plains of the Wateree and Congaree, also had flooded the approach to Nelson's Ferry lower on the Santee (Boland, 2004). Greene had to move an army of more than 2000 troops, infantry and cavalry as well as field pieces and baggage, across the Santee

River in the most expeditious manner. Nelson's Ferry would not be suitable (Boland, 2004).

A tactical consideration may have presented an even stronger argument against attempting a crossing on the Santee. With Lt. Col. Stewart still at his position close to Fort Motte and other British troops in Dorchester and Charleston, a crossing at Nelson's Ferry would have put Greene's army between those forces. Greene's entire strategy required him to always keep his route open to his supply line and a safe route in case of a need to retreat.

Another option was to move north on the Wateree and ferry the army across that river. Then move down the south side to the Congaree and cross that river above the British post. This would keep his route free to the mountains to the west in case he needed to retreat to Virginia (Lee, 1812). It would require a longer march for his troops but would be less hazardous. Also, the troops of Pickens and Henderson were on the Congaree and he wished to have them join him before an attack (Lee, 1812).

On 23 August 1781 Nathanael Greene's army set out at five in the morning. Part of the Sumner's North Carolina troops led the way, the rest of the North Carolinians were at the back, herding the beeves (cattle) which would provide food for the march. By marching in the early morning and late afternoon, Greene could preserve the strength of his army. Although it was early September, it was still a season of intense heat in the Carolinas. The army proceeded by slow marches toward Camden. When the army was halted, they practiced firing blank ammunition as the greatest weakness in commanding raw recruits was their habit of firing without orders (Rankin, 1971).

At Camden, Greene established a hospital for those who had become ill on the march. Those who recovered sufficiently were to follow. He then crossed the Wateree River in the vicinity of Camden and moved down towards

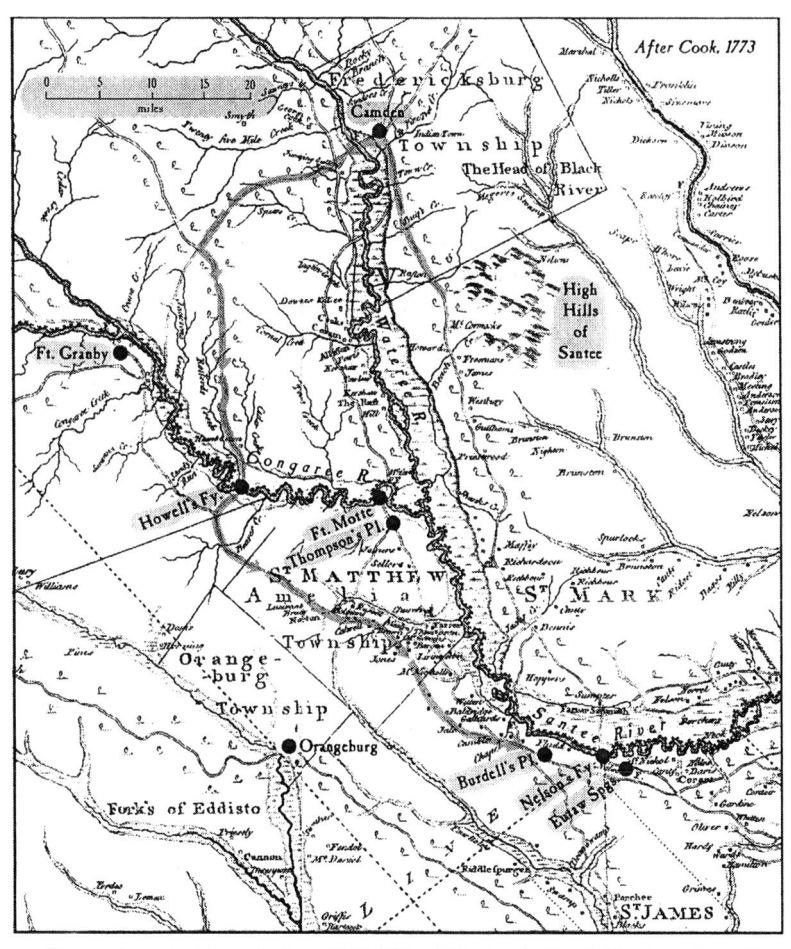

Greene's probable route from High Hills of Santee to Burdell's plantation. It is known that he crossed the Wateree in the vicinity of Camden and that he crossed the Congaree at Howell's Ferry. It is presumed that he followed the major roads.

the Congaree (Lee, 1812). As he neared Friday's Ferry on the Congaree on 27 August, Greene learned that Lt. Col. Stewart was no longer at Colonel Thomson's plantation near McCord's Ferry, but had moved down the Santee River and now encamped at Eutaw Springs which was about 40 miles south of Greene's position (N. Greene's report to George Washington in Gibbes).

Greene determined to cross the Congaree River at Howell's Ferry, upstream from Friday's Ferry, as that location would put him close to the protection of Fort Granby. It was here that he was joined by Pickens and Henderson.

On 5 September, Greene left his heavy baggage at Howell's Ferry, keeping only two wagons loaded with hospital supplies and rum (Lee, 1812). It was on this date that Greene heard of Marion's successful ambush of Major Fraser at Parker's Ferry (Lee, 1812).

Although Greene was still moving by short, slow marches because of the oppressive heat, he reported that he wished to give Marion an opportunity to join him. For this reason he stopped at Fort Motte, then moved to Laurens plantation where he stopped before moving to Burdell's plantation just seven miles upriver from the British at Eutaw Springs. It was during this time that Marion joined him after moving his men around the British camp. Marion had been on the same side of the Santee River as the British, and camped downstream at Peyre's Plantation.

With Marion's arrival Greene's army was complete and on the night of 7 September Greene's army rested. Since Greene had made no attempt to disguise his intentions he assumed that Stewart was aware of his presence, but records indicate that Stewart was not. The British camp slept just seven miles down river unaware that Greene and his army were already so close to Eutaw Springs.

As Lee reported:

The same dead calm continued: nobody was even seen moving in any direction- a state of quiet never before experienced in similar circumstances. While Stewart spent the night perfectly at ease, from his ignorance of passing events, the American general was preparing for battle. (Lee, 1821:465).

CHAPTER V

GREENE'S AMERICAN ARMY

As Greene moved toward Eutaw Springs he had the best army he could muster but it was far short of what he would have wished. After his bitter criticism of militia at Guilford Courthouse, he was forced to use them here. He had no choice. One third of his army was militia. Would this army be equal to the task ahead?

The Americans, as did the British, used a variety of military organizations during the Revolutionary War. There were three major categories depending upon the men comprising the military organization.

The Continental Army was authorized by Congress on 14 June 1775 after the first incident of the Revolution at Lexington and Concord. The following day, 15 June 1775, George Washington was chosen, unanimously, as the commander of all continental forces (Wright, 1989). Since the inhabitants who had previous military service had been members of the British forces during the French and Indian War (Seven Years War), it is no surprise that the organization of the army was fashioned after the British system. Further, the tactics were those of European troops. The period of enlistment was three years and that was considered a generous amount of time to deal with the present troubles. This proved not to be the case and, by the time of the Southern Campaign, many of the units were far below full strength.

State troops were usually enlisted for six to eighteen months (Babits, 1998). Some men who had previously been enlisted in the Continental Army would join state troops especially when bounties were paid. In some instances men of wealth would hire others to serve in their stead. By the time of the Southern Campaign many of the soldiers in the state troop units had seen considerable action.

Militia had served in the colonies from the beginning of settlement. Every male was responsible for the defense of the colony so most of the population had, at one time or another, been involved in the militia. They had mustered periodically and had served when necessary. Militia had been used to fight in the Indian territory, and, in the south, to control slaves. Since few men were exempt from this service, it provided men accustomed to firearms. It had been militiamen who had engaged the British troops at Lexington and Concord (Wright, 1989). Early on the militia contained both men who would support independence and those who would support the king. As the conflict became more clearly defined, the Tories who supported the king were eliminated from the patriot, or Whig, units (Babits, 1998). These Tories were, in South Carolina, organized by the British into Loyalist militia units.

The troops which Major General Nathanael Greene had under his command as he approached Eutaw Springs were a mixture of Continentals, state troops and militia. Many units had considerable experience.

CONTINENTALS

Maryland Continentals. Colonel Otho Williams commanded two battalions of the Maryland Continentals, numbering about 250 (Lumpkin, 1981). One battalion was commanded by Lieutenant Colonel John Eager Howard, a hero of the Battle of Cowpens. The other battalion was commanded by Major Henry Hardman.

The Maryland Continentals were a seasoned group. Some had served since the beginning of the hostilities and would serve to the end (Babits, 1998). They were lead by outstanding officers, especially Colonel Otho Williams. Active in the Northern campaign, Williams had been taken prisoner by the Hessians when Fort Washington fell. However, after the surrender of the British troops at Saratoga, Williams was exchanged for a British officer and assumed command of a Maryland Regiment. After the British occupied Charleston, Williams accompanied Baron de Kalb south and, when General Gates arrived to take command, Williams was appointed deputy adjutant-general. After the defeat at Camden, he attempted to rebuild the shattered Continental Army. When Major General Nathanael Greene assumed command, Williams would serve as adjutant-general. In this position he was second in command of the Southern forces.

After the Battle of Cowpens which occurred while Williams was stationed at Greene's headquarters at Hicks Creek (Wallace, South Carolina), Williams accompanied the troops in the 'Race to the Dan' (Buchanan, 1997). He assumed command of Morgan's Flying Army when Morgan became too ill to continue. Second in command at the battle of Guilford Courthouse, Siege of Ninety-Six and Hobkirk's Hill, he would continue to serve until the hostilities ceased (Lee, 1812).

Another Maryland officer of unquestioned courage and capabilities was Lt. Col. John Eager Howard, a hero of the Battle of Cowpens (Babits, 1998). For his service at that battle, where he commanded the Continental infantry, Congress awarded him a silver medal (Buchanan, 1997). Although not successful at Guilford Courthouse, the Siege of Ninety-Six, or Hobkirk's Hill, he still executed his command with bravery (Lee, 1812), and Greene had the utmost confidence in this young officer.

Virginia Continentals. Lieutenant Colonel Richard Campbell commanded two battalions of Virginia Continentals, numbering about 250 men (Lumpkin, 1981). The battalions were commanded by Major Sneed and Captain Thomas Edmonds.

Virginia Continentals had joined Greene before the engagement at Guilford Courthouse, and fought there, at Hobkirk Hill's, and the Siege of Ninety-Six. Again, these men were experienced and could be depended upon to stand fast against British soldiers.

Delaware Continentals. (Kirkwood's Company). Commanded by Captain Robert Kirkwood the company numbered 60-70 (Lumpkin, 1981). The Delawares, under the command of Captain Kirkwood, had fought in the American victory against Banastre Tarleton at Cowpens. Many of his men there had fought at the terrible American defeat at Camden and were experienced in the British conduct of battle (Babits, 1998). Kirkwood's Company was involved in the Battle of Guilford Courthouse (Buchanan, 1997), the Battle of Hobkirk's Hill, and the Siege of Ninety-Six.

Major General Nathanael Greene had reason to be confident of the abilities of the Continentals of Maryland, Virginia and Delaware. They had faced the British Army in the field and had exchanged volley for volley, and countered bayonet charge with bayonet charge. They were combat ready.

The North Carolina Continentals were a different story.

North Carolina Continentals. General Jethro Sumner commanded three battalions of North Carolina Continentals numbering about 350 men (Lumpkin, 1981). The battalions were commanded by Colonel Ashe, Major Armstrong and Major Blount. The original North Carolina regiments had fought in the defense of Philadelphia and in battles from Philadelphia to Monmouth Courthouse. From there they were reassigned to the Southern Department and had been taken prisoner by the British after the fall of Charleston (Wright, 1989).

The present regiments were reorganized in the summer of 1781 and nine companies were to be assigned to the Southern Department, under the command of Major General Nathanael Greene (Wright, 1989). General Jethro Sumner was assigned the task of reforming the North Carolina Continentals in that state, but the presence of Lord Cornwallis in the area made recruiting difficult.

Sumner's task was further complicated by smallpox epidemics in Halifax (NC) and Hillsborough (NC) making it dangerous to assemble the drafted troops (Rankin, 1971). The failure of Virginia to provide drafts and/or arms delayed the movement of the companies toward Greene (Schenck, 1889). Also, the fear that Lord Cornwallis would return his infantry to Charleston by sea and send his cavalry back through North Carolina made General Sumner uneasy. Finally, with the arrival of muskets from LaFayette (Schenck,1889), the North Carolinians were able to proceed to the High Hills of the Santee where Greene was encamped. Here, the newly formed companies were drilled and trained in the ways of battle (Schenck, 1889). The question of whether or not these Continentals were 'battle ready' would be answered at Eutaw Springs.

CAVALRY

Greene's army included two units of cavalry commanded by Lt. Col. Henry Lee and Lt. Col. William Washington.

Lee's Legion. Commanded by Lt. Col. Henry Lee, the Legion numbered about 60 cavalry and 100 infantry (Lumpkin, 1981). Lee's Partisan Corps consisted, at this time, of three mounted troops (cavalry) and three dismounted troops (infantry). They had been assigned to the Southern Department on 31 October 1780 (Wright, 1989), after seeing action in New Jersey, Philadelphia and New York. After joining Greene at Hicks Creek (Wallace, South Carolina) in December 1780, Lt. Col. Lee was dispatched to the swamps of the Pee Dee where he campaigned with militia Brigadier General Francis Marion.

After being recalled to accompany Greene's Army in the 'Race to the Dan', and Guilford Courthouse, Lee was again dispatched to combine forces with Marion to capture Fort Watson and Fort Motte. Next, Lee joined militia leaders Andrew Pickens and Elijah Clarke and moved to Augusta, Georgia. After that British garrison fell, Lee again joined Greene at Ninety-Six and accompanied Greene's army across South Carolina to the High Hills of the Santee. This corps, along with Washington's cavalry, moved along the area moving supplies out of reach of the enemy and providing intelligence for the Americans.

Virginia Continental Cavalry. This cavalry was commanded by Lt. Col. William Washington and numbered about 80 (Lumpkin, 1981). This unit, too, had a history of exemplary service. William Washington was a second cousin (once removed) to General George Washington, the Commander of the Continental Army. William had entered the beginning of the hostilities and served bravely at the Battle of Trenton. When General Washington was able to form a cavalry, William was transferred to that service since he was an excellent horseman and had already demonstrated the qualities of leadership (Haller, 2001). After serving in the Brandywine and Germantown battles, he moved his unit to the Charleston area in the summer of 1780 (Haller, 2001). His unit was engaged in this area until after the fall of Charleston, and the disastrous Battle of Camden. He then moved his unit to North Carolina as Major General Gates attempted to rebuild his shattered Continental Army.

When Major General Nathanael Greene assumed command of the Continental Army in December of 1780, Washington's cavalry accompanied Brigadier General Daniel Morgan's Flying Army in his campaign in western Carolina. At the Battle of Cowpens, 17 January 1781, Washington met his old adversary, Lt. Col. Banastre Tarleton and his British Legion. For his conspicuous bravery at Cowpens, Congress awarded him a silver medal. As the Continental Army moved, north in the 'Race to the Dan', Washington's cavalry accompanied them. Turning back southward, Washington's cavalry served at Guilford Courthouse, Hobkirk's Hill and Ninety-Six.

Lee and Washington were now in the field providing reconnaissance and harassing the enemy. Greene referred to Lee as his eyes, and Washington as his arm.

Artillery. The artillery consisted of two three-pounders commanded by Captain William Gaines and two six-pounders commanded by Captain Browne or Captain Finn (Lumpkin, 1981).

STATE TROOPS

South Carolina State Troops. Commanded by Lieutenant Colonels William Henderson and Wade Hampton the troops consisted of about 72 cavalry and 73 infantry (Lumpkin, 1981). Shortly after the Battle of Guilford Courthouse, Governor Rutledge of South Carolina authorized militia Brigadier General Thomas Sumter to raise a brigade of State troops "for the term of ten months, each man to find his own clothing, horse, arms and equipment, but to be found in forage and rations by the public, and receive a grown negro(sic) for his pay" (Schenck, 1889:441). Many of the men in these units were recruited from the area between the Yadkin and Catawba Rivers in North Carolina.

At the time Greene was assembling his troops to campaign against Lt. Col. Stewart, Thomas Sumter was conspicuously absent. Greene had lost confidence after Sumter's failures to support Morgan's forces at Cowpens, to join Greene before Hobkirk's Hill, and to prevent Lord Rawdon from reaching Ninety-Six. Sumter's command at Quimby Bridge, which resulted in heavy casualties in Marion's Brigade and in Lee's Legion, had infuriated both Marion and Lee and they had determined that their men would never again fight under Sumter's command (Lee, 1812). Now, as troops were being assembled, the state troops and the militia which Thomas Sumter had recruited were present, but Thomas Sumter was not.

MILITIA

The South Carolina Militia consisted of a combined force of Brigadier General Thomas Sumter's and Brigadier General Andrew Pickens' Brigades. It numbered about 370 and was commanded by Andrew Pickens. Sumter's militia had been active in the midlands of South Carolina since the initiation of the Southern Campaign. They had fought Tories and British regulars at Brattonsville, Rocky Mount, Hanging Rock, Fishing Creek, and Blackstock's. Although not always successful they had inflicted severe damage on their enemy. Andrew Pickens' own militia were men of the back country and many had fought at Musgrove's Mill, King's Mountain and Cowpens.

When Brigadier General Daniel Morgan needed support, at Cowpens, militia Colonel Andrew Pickens had called out the back country militia and they had responded to his call and mustered about a thousand riflemen at Cowpens. Their aimed volleys had decimated the British line (Babits, 1998). Congress awarded Pickens a sword for his gallantry at Cowpens.

Andrew Pickens had followed the Continental Army into North Carolina and had served courageously there. When Greene began his campaign to take back the South

Carolina territory, he depended on Andrew Pickens to participate and he did. Lt. Col. Lee, with Pickens and the Georgia militia under the command of Lt. Col. Elijah Clarke, had forced the surrender of the British at Augusta. Pickens was a stern man who, it is said, rarely spoke and never smiled, but he was a commander whose troops respected him and Greene had the utmost confidence in his leadership.

Marion's Brigade was commanded by Brigadier General Francis Marion and included about 40 cavalry and 200 infantry (Lumpkin, 1981). Francis Marion, the Swamp Fox, had been an officer in the South Carolina Continental Army and fought at Sullivan's Island (Fort Moultrie) and Savannah. His unit, the 2nd South Carolina Continental Line, was captured by the British Army at Charleston. Marion escaped capture since he had broken an ankle and had been evacuated before the surrender.

When the British occupied the entire state, Marion took command of the Williamsburg militia and carried on a guerilla war in the swamps of the Santee and Pee Dee Rivers. In a series of encounters at Nelson's Ferry (25 August 1780), Blue Savannah (4 September 1780), Black Mingo (28-29 September 1780), Tearcoat Swamp (25 October 1780, Halfway Swamp and Singleton's Mill (13 December 1780), Georgetown (24-25 January 1781), Wyboo Swamp (6 March 1781), Mount Hope Swamp, Lower Bridge of the Black River (March 1781), Sampit Bridge (28 March 1781), Fort Watson (15-23 April 1781), Fort Motte (8-12 May 1781), and Quimby Bridge (17 July 1781) he embarrassed the British regulars and intimidated the Tories who supported them (Lumpkin, 1981). A small, taciturn, introverted man, he had eluded five commanders the British had sent into the swamp to 'neutralize' him.

When Major General Nathanael Greene turned his army back into South Carolina, Francis Marion coordinated his efforts to implement Greene's strategies. Even as Greene had assembled his army in the High Hills, Marion had moved into the Pon Pon area (Edisto) and ambushed the South Carolina Royalists under Major Fraser. Marion was a commander upon whom Greene could depend.

North Carolina Militia. Colonel Francis Malmedy commanded a unit of about 150 men (Lumpkin, 1981). "They were chiefly new men called up for the campaign and commanded by Colonel Malmedy, a foreign officer personally unknown to his soldiers" (Lumpkin, 1981:217). Also, since Malmedy had performed poorly at the defense of Charleston and both General Washington and General Greene considered him a troublemaker, he was an unlikely choice for command of the North Carolina militia.

General Greene had ordered the militia, under Shelby and Sevier, from the mountains of western North Carolina to join him but Indian attacks in their territory made that impossible. Many of that militia had fought at Musgrove's Mill, King's Mountain and many other up country encounters. They had experience and had demonstrated tremendous courage in battle. They would have been a welcome addition to this army.

Greene had expected one other militia group, about 150 men of the Georgia Refugees, commanded by Lt. Col. Elijah Clarke and Major James McCall. The Georgians had been active since the beginning of the British occupation at Kettle Creek, Musgrove's Mill, Blackstock's, and many other smaller skirmishes. At the Battle of Cowpens (17 January 1781) 75 Georgians had manned the skirmish line and their sharpshooters had inflicted many casualties on Tarleton's British Legion dragoons. The mounted militia at Cowpens had been commanded by Major James McCall.

Unfortunately, the Georgians had been struck down with smallpox in April. Fifty had died of the disease, among those was Major James McCall, a hero of Kettle Creek, Musgrove's Mill, Hammond's Store and Cowpens.

Although Elijah Clarke survived , his Georgia Refugees had been decimated by death and disease and therefore were not able to make the long trip in the summer heat.

These were the units moving against Lt. Col. Stewart's British army. The total number of troops commanded by Major General Nathanael Greene at the Battle of Eutaw Springs was about 2100, of which 1900 would be engaged (Lumpkin, 1981).

(A definitive listing of participants is available in Volume Three of *Nothing but Blood and Slaughter* by Patrick O'Kelley, published in 2005.)

CHAPTER VI

THE BRITISH ARMY

Lt. Col. Alexander Stewart (See Endnote 3), who had assumed command of the British Army after the departure of Lord Rawdon, was an officer in the 3rd Regiment of Foot. Lt. Col. Stewart had arrived in Charleston on 3 June 1781 with the 3rd, the 19th and the 30th Regiments of Foot. These British regulars had previously been stationed in Ireland.

Encamped on the property of patriot militia Colonel Thomson, about a mile down river from Fort Motte, Stewart was concerned about the welfare of his troops. Their supplies were low and the men were suffering from the heat and humidity of a South Carolina summer. The decision was made to move. The circumstances which led to the move were articulated in a report to Lord Cornwallis in which Lt. Col. Stewart gave his account of the battle. It was written at Eutaw, 9 September 1781 (Lieutenant Colonel Stewart to Earl Cornwallis in Lee, 1812).

Stewart reported that Greene's army was on the move and, due to the flooded conditions of the swamps and rivers, had moved to Camden and had crossed the Wateree River and was presumed to be moving toward Friday's Ferry on the Congaree. However, Stewart had little accurate intelligence as he reports that the rebels had controlled the "by-ways and passes through the different swamps". His estimation of Greene's force to be 4,000 men is certainly evidence that his intelligence was faulty since, when Greene had left the High Hills of the Santee, he had fewer than half that number.

Stewart explained his lack of supplies and, since Major McArthur was moving supplies from Charleston toward him, he suggested that if he were to move a detachment toward the supply convoy and meet them at Martin's Tavern in Ferguson's Swamp, it would require a march of fifty-six miles and a detachment of four hundred men since Greene's superior number of cavalry would pose a threat to a smaller detachment. Therefore, Stewart chose to move his entire army toward the Eutaws by slow marches (Lee, 1812).

Although Stewart believed Greene's force to be about twice the size of his own, he certainly should have had great confidence in the forces he commanded.

During the Revolutionary War, the British had, at their disposal, a variety of troops:

British Regulars: The British Army had many units which were part of the standing army. These units were raised, for the most part, in the British Isles and many of the regular units were involved in this war. These soldiers were well trained professionals and were considered at the time to be the best trained soldiers in the world. After the war most of the men in these units returned to England, Ireland or Scotland.

British Provincials. Once in this country, Great Britain enlisted men loyal to the mother country into what were termed provincial units. These men were uniformed, paid and equipped by England and were full-time soldiers. The units were mostly recruited in the northern colonies, many from the New York and New Jersey area, where the inhabitants were fiercely loyal to King George. Many of these units were transferred to the south during the Southern

Campaign and fought extensively from Savannah to Yorktown. After the war many were relocated in Nova Scotia, Canada, as they were unwelcome in the new independent nation. (See Endnote 4).

Loyalist Militia. Once troops were moved from New England and the Middle States to Georgia and the Carolinas, the British occupation forces organized local Loyalists into what they termed "Loyalist militia." Patriots refer to them as "Tory militia." These units were composed of citizen soldiers who were paid and supplied by the British. They mustered when called out but were part-time combatants. The intent was that the British army would win the battles and take the territory, then move on while the local Loyalists held the territory and kept the rebels in check. There were many of these militia groups in the southern colonies. (See Endnote 5)

Foreign Nationals. Since the British regular army was stretched over several fronts, the British government hired armies from European princes. These units are often referred to as "Hessian" but there were many units in addition to those from Hesse-Cassel. There were approximately 30,000 of these foreign soldiers involved in the Revolutionary War.

Since the departure of Lord Rawdon, Lt. Col. Stewart commanded a British force of British regulars and provincial units. He had no local militia units or foreign troops with him. The units of British regulars were: the 3rd Regiment of Foot; the 63rd Regiment of Foot; the 64th Regiment of Foot; the 84th Regiment of Foot, and six flank companies, two each (light infantry and grenadiers) of the 3rd, 19th and 30th Regiments of Foot. The 3rd, 19th and 30th Regiments had recently arrived from Ireland (Lumpkin, 1981). The artillery was served by Royal Artillerymen who were regulars.

Provincial units at Eutaw Springs were: one battalion of

DeLancey's New York Brigade; one battalion of New Jersey Volunteers; one battalion of New York Volunteers; one troop of cavalry from the South Carolina Regiment of Royalists (Lumpkin, 1981).

BRITISH REGULARS

3rd Regiment of Foot. The regiment had been posted in Cork, Ireland, and consisted mostly of Irish citizens. When the three regiments, 3rd, 19th and 30th Regiments of Foot, set sail for America they were intended to join Lord Cornwallis as he was campaigning in Virginia. However, communications between Cornwallis and Charleston were intercepted and the troops disembarked at Charleston. The flank companies of the regiments had been marched to the relief of Ninety-Six. Although new to the American colonies they were, nonetheless, well trained regular British troops.

63rd Regiment of Foot. This regiment arrived in Boston in June, 1775. Their flank companies (grenadiers and light infantry companies) fought at Bunker Hill. Detachments of the regiment saw action in Newport, New York and Philadelphia. They were engaged at the last large battle in the north, the Battle of Monmouth Courthouse, where they faced many of the Americans who would be their adversaries at Eutaw Springs. Moved to the south, they were engaged at the Siege of Charleston. Detachments were used to keep the supply lines open between Charleston and Camden and fought at Fishdam Ford, SC; Blackstock's, SC; Hobkirk's Hill, SC; and finally, at Eutaw Springs (Katcher, 1973).

64th Regiment of Foot. The regiment arrived in Boston in January of 1769 but was diverted to Halifax for three years. The regiment returned to Boston in 1772 commanded by Lt. Col. Leslie. The unit remained in the environs of Boston until the Revolutionary War started. The regiment then was engaged in New York at Long Island, and at Philadelphia,

Brandywine and Germantown. Their last engagement in the north was at the Battle of Monmouth Courthouse where they faced Americans whom they would face again at Eutaw Springs. Sent to the south to siege Charleston in December of 1779, the regiment remained there until the end of the war (Katcher, 1973). Detachments were involved in accompanying convoys and replacements from Charleston to other British outposts. A detachment accompanied Lt. Col. John Watson as he pursued Francis Marion's brigade through the area between the Santee and Georgetown in March of 1781 and had suffered several casualties in those encounters. A detachment of the 64th had been defending Fort Watson when it was sieged and taken by Brigadier General Francis Marion and Lt. Col. Henry (Light Horse Harry) Lee in April of 1781.

84th Regiment of Foot (Royal Highland Emigrants). The regiment was raised in Canada from veterans of disbanded Highland regiments. It was raised as a provincial unit but was transferred to regular status in January 1779. The second battalion had been at the British attempt to take Charleston, South Carolina in 1776 but had been returned to the northern states when that attempt failed. There they had fought in the Philadelphia Campaign, at Brandywine, Germantown and Monmouth Courthouse. They were moved to Maine and Nova Scotia to combat privateers, and returned to New York. They were again sent to Charleston during the Southern Campaign. Detachments had served in South Carolina, the latest being the defense of Fort Motte which had been captured by Marion and Lee.

Flank Companies of the 3rd, 19th and 30th Regiments of Foot. The "flank companies" of a regiment were light infantry and grenadiers. The light infantry was a corps of skirmishers and was an elite group of soldiers. The grenadiers had, in the 1600's wars, thrown grenades at the enemy. The size and weight of the missile required tall and muscular soldiers. Although the British army no longer used grenades during the Revolutionary War, they continued the tradition of the grenadiers into the 1700's and the British Grenadiers were respected and feared by their enemies. One might equate them with today's United States Special Forces.

The three regiments with their flank companies had been sent from England to Cork, Ireland in 1775. Many of the soldiers in these units were Irish. By the spring of 1781 British forces in the Carolinas needed reinforcements. Engagements such as King's Mountain and Cowpens had cost dearly and local Tories were not enthusiastic about replacing British losses. Three regiments were shipped from Ireland in March 1781 and landed at the port of Charleston in June. The six flank companies of the three regiments accompanied Lord Rawdon in his relief of Ninety-Six. These troops, recently arrived from the cool weather of Ireland and clad in woolen uniforms, suffered greatly on that march. It is reported that fifty died of heat and related complications.

On 17 July 1781 the 19th Regiment of Foot, without the services of the flank company which was serving with Lord Rawdon, fought under Col. Coates at Quinby Bridge against the combined forces of Sumter, Marion and Lee. Although the 19th maintained the field, they abandoned the position during the night and retreated to Monck's Corner. At Eutaw Springs the flank companies were commanded by Major John Marjoribanks, an officer in the 19th Regiment of Foot. (See Endnote 6).

Artillery. The British had three six-pound cannon and one four-pound cannon (Lumpkin, 1981). Those guns were served by a detachment of Royal Artillery whose troops were assigned to the guns and served where needed.

The units of British regulars commanded by Lt. Col. Stewart had fought extensively in the north and in the south.

Although they had sustained many casualties they were highly trained and well experienced. With the exception of the recent arrivals from Ireland, they had seen long months of service in the Carolinas.

The provincial units Colonel Stewart had at his disposal were no less experienced.

PROVINCIAL REGULARS

One Battalion of DeLancey's New York Brigade. This unit of provincial regulars was commanded by Lieutenant Colonel John Harris Cruger. A highly regarded Loyalist, he was second in command and, had Stewart become incapacitated, Cruger would have taken command. Authorized in September of 1776 DeLancey's was raised with Loyalists in New York, a very strong pro-British area. The units were charged with the defense of Long Island. In October 1778, two battalions were ordered to Savannah where they saw action at both the capture of Savannah and later, when the Americans attempted to retake the city.

In July 1780 the first battalion of DeLancey's and the 3rd Battalion of New Jersey Volunteers were ordered to Ninety-Six, a major British outpost from which the British attempted to control the upcountry (Katcher, 1973). Cruger commanded this post and, during the summer of 1781, had defended the fort for a month against the American forces, commanded by Major General Nathanael Greene, until Lord Rawdon could come to his aid. When the British evacuated Ninety-Six, Cruger was responsible for the removal of all troops, stores, and Loyalist civilians to Charleston. In John Cruger, Stewart had an able commander.

Third Battalion of New Jersey Volunteers. In some accounts (Lumpkin, 1981) the commander of this battalion of provincial regulars is listed as Major Joseph Greene but the unit historians name Isaac Allen as the commander at the time of Eutaw Springs. The unit had been sent to Savannah with deLancey's Brigade and transferred to Ninety-Six with that same group. Lt. Col. Allen shared the command with Lt. Col. Cruger and it was here that the New Jersey Volunteers saw considerable action (Katcher, 1973). They had accompanied Col. Innes of the South Carolina Royalists into an ambush at Musgrove's Mill.

The unit had a long association with Major Patrick Ferguson before the movement of the units to the south so many volunteered to accompany Ferguson in his campaign to pacify the back country of South Carolina. Those men, Ferguson's Rangers, were lost at King's Mountain. After the evacuation of Ninety-Six the remaining members of the New Jersey Volunteers accompanied Lt. Col. Stewart in his campaign along the Santee River which ended at Eutaw Springs.

One Battalion of New York Volunteers. This unit of provincial regulars also had seen considerable action in the Southern Campaign. They had participated in both actions at Savannah, and at Charleston (Katcher, 1973). Moved to the interior, they were posted at Ninety-Six where detachments had participated in skirmishes with patriot militia.

This unit, also, had a long association with Major Patrick Ferguson and some had volunteered to accompany him as Ferguson's Rangers. Those who joined Ferguson were lost at King's Mountain. Before the siege of Ninety-Six the New York Volunteers had been moved to Camden to provide more security for Lord Rawdon. They were engaged in the Battle of Hobkirk's Hill and, with Lord Rawdon, evacuated Camden after that battle. At Eutaw Springs they were commanded by Major Sheridan.

South Carolina Regiment of Loyalists. This unit is more properly named South Carolina Royalists. The South Carolina Royalists was a provincial unit organized in East Florida from Loyalist refugees from South Carolina in 1778 (Lambert, 1987). The unit was active around Charleston during the British siege of that city. A detachment under Col. Innes was caught in heavy fire from the patriots at Musgrove's Mill. For the most part, the regiment was active in the low country of South Carolina, and saw considerable action in the vicinity of Ninety-Six. At Eutaw Springs they were commanded by Major John Coffin, a cavalry officer from Massachusetts, who had come south with the New York Volunteers (Lambert, 1987). He had commanded several cavalry units in other engagements, such as the New York Dragoons at the Battle of Hobkirk's Hill. Coffin continued to serve with the cavalry units of the Royalists.

The South Carolina Royalists had, under the command of Major Thomas Fraser, captured Col. Isaac Hayne and turned him over to British headquarters in Charleston. Col. Balfour and Lord Rawdon had Col. Hayne hanged hoping to intimidate the patriot opposition. In retaliation, Patriot leader Brigadier General Francis Marion (the Swamp Fox) had ambushed Major Fraser and his mounted on the causeway to Parker's Ferry about two weeks before the Battle of Eutaw Springs. Marion had estimated that he had inflicted about one hundred casualties, killed or wounded, on the Royalists (Bass 1974; Rankin 1973). Major Frazer was reported wounded in the ambush (Frierson, 1999). The Jarvis account states that one hundred and twenty-five were killed and many more wounded. Although the numbers of casualties reported varies, it was a significant loss, and certainly decreased the strength of cavalry available to the British in the low country and possibly to Colonel Stewart at Eutaw Springs

The units had suffered many casualties in the months they had been serving in South Carolina and Georgia. Not only were wounds slow to heal, but infections killed many of the wounded. In addition to the acts of war, malaria, smallpox, dysentery, typhoid, yellow fever, heat stroke and snake and insect bites had taken their toll to the point that some writers referred to Stewart's units as "remnants." Their ranks had been thinned by adversity but those remaining were seasoned, experienced troops. The roughly 2000 men were a formidable group. Although Stewart would report to Lord Cornwallis that he had faced a superior force, the British had the advantage in numbers of experienced and disciplined troops.

CHAPTER VII

THE BATTLE

Although Lt. Col. Stewart knew that Greene's army was moving, he did not believe that the Americans would attack without militia general Francis Marion and Stewart reported that Marion was at the Pon Pon (Indian name for the Edisto River). Since Marion's whereabouts had not been known until after the ambush on Fraser, Stewart must have known about the loss of Fraser's dragoons. What he appears not to have known is the rapidity with which Marion could move his brigade: Marion's mounted brigade could cover fifty miles through the swamps at night (Lumpkin, 1981), and they were already back at Peyre's Plantation on the Santee River.

Col. Stewart had moved his men slowly toward Eutaw Springs. Here cold water surfaced from two springs and formed a creek or branch which flowed through a steep gully to the Santee River.

> Near the head of the creek stood Patrick Roche' fine brick mansion house of two stories and an attic, looking out over a cleared area of some eight acres. The clearing

before the house was bisected by the east-west river road, one branch of which, just beyond the house, split off toward Charleston, sixty miles away. A pallisaded garden lay between the mansion and the creek. Little undergrowth grew beneath the great oaks and cypresses in the woods surrounding the open area. (Rankin, 1973:241).

The clearing spanned the River Road and included an Indian mound which Otho Williams suggested was a burial place of Indians who had died fighting a battle in that place about a century before (Williams in Gibbes, 1873). Actually the mounds in South Carolina, built by Mississippi or Woodlands Mound Builders, predated by many generations the Indians which the first white settlers encountered in the area.

Behind the house and at the edge of the springs was a pallisaded garden. Also, on the property were outbuildings and a barn. About a mile down river from the springs the road from Charleston to Camden crossed the Santee River at Nelson's Ferry.

Here Stewart and his army would wait in relative comfort for the supplies which Major McArthur would bring up the River Road from Monck's Corner.

At four o'clock in the morning of 8 September 1781 Major General Nathanael Greene started his march towards Eutaw Springs. The army marched in two columns with artillery at the head of each. Lt. Col. Henry Lee was positioned in the front and Lt. Col. William Washington in the rear (Lee, 1812).

In spite of the fact that two North Carolinians had deserted from the American Army during the night and had appeared in the British camp at Eutaw Springs, Lt. Col.

Stewart was evidently unaware of Greene's approach. He sent out 'rooting parties' from each unit to gather sweet potatoes to compensate for the lack of bread. In his report to Lord Cornwallis, Lt. Col. Stewart explained that "the flank companies and the buffs, having gone too far in front, fell into the enemy's hands before the action began." (Stewart's report to Cornwallis in Lee, 1812:605). But it was not only Buffs, the 3rd Regiment of Foot, from the rooting party who were taken prisoner as the history of the 64th Regiment of Foot indicated that of 100 men taken prisoner, an ensign and sixty-two rank and file, were from that unit (Urwin, nd).

However, Lt. Col. Stewart did dispatch Major Coffin "with one hundred and forty infantry and fifty cavalry, in order to gain intelligence of the enemy." (Lt. Col. Stewart's report to Lord Cornwallis in Lee, 1812:604).

Major Coffin's patrol encountered the American van at about eight o'clock in the morning and about 4 miles from the British camp (Lee, 1812). Believing that he had encountered a militia patrol of the American army, Coffin attacked. Lee's Legion and Henderson's Corp met the charge and the British were beaten back. The British infantry suffered heavy casualties and forty were taken prisoner. The British cavalry fled and gave the alarm to the camp. The rooting party was also alerted at this time and as many as could returned to the British camp although many of their armed guard were taken prisoner.

Lt. Col. Stewart, now aware of the proximity of the Greene's army, alerted his men who were still at breakfast. He established his line of defense about 200 yards in front of his headquarters and camp which were located in the house and cleared fields on both sides of the road. James states that the line was a mile from the springs (James, 1821). O'Kelley's account would support the farther distance. He reports that the American line encountered the British

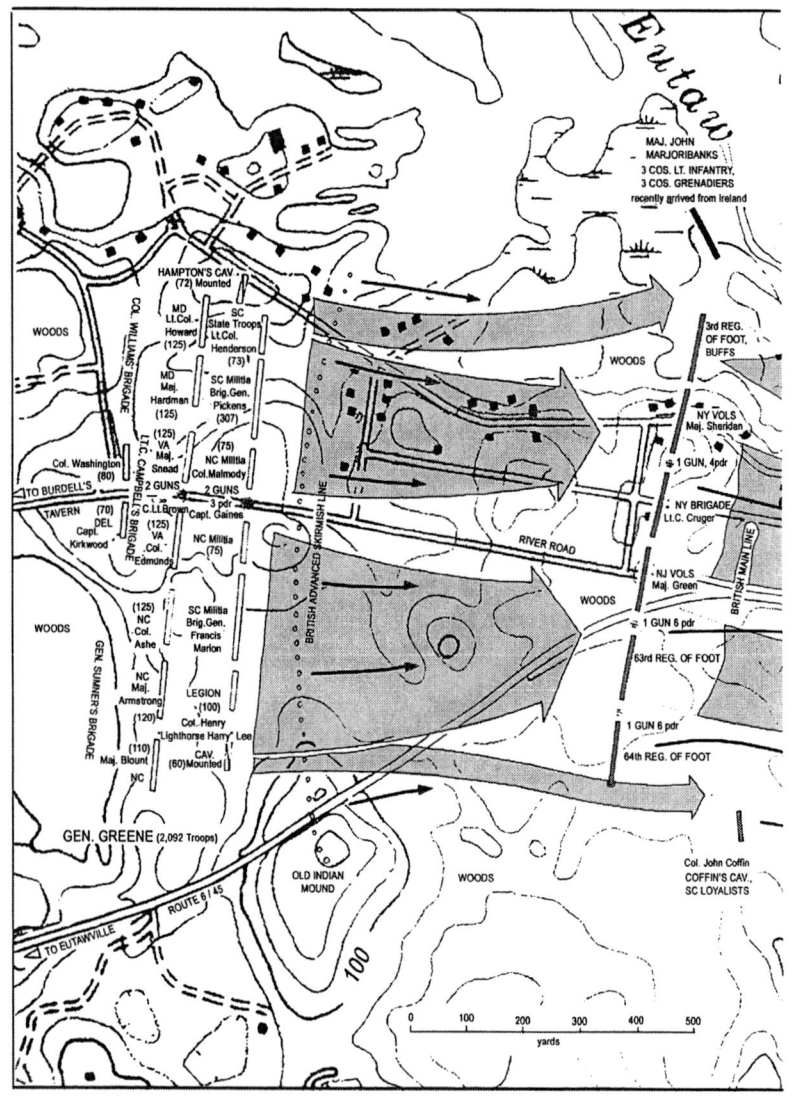

Map of the Battle of Eutaw Springs by David Reuwer.
Used by permission

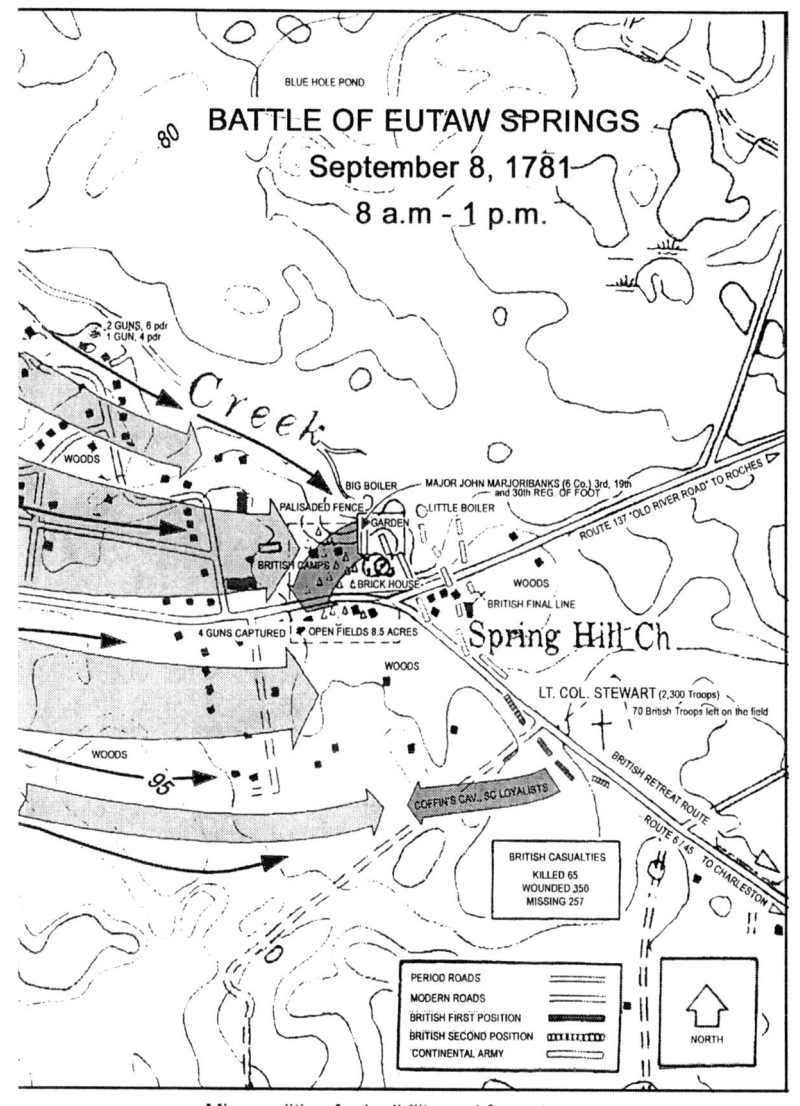

Minor editing for legibility and format.

skirmishers about 2 miles from the British camp (O'Kelley, 2005). The area where the line of battle was established was in a wooded area and is described as forested with great oaks and cypress trees with little undergrowth.

To the right of the British line, in a thicket beside the creek which ran from the springs to the Santee River, Major John Marjoribanks commanded a force of flank companies of the 3rd, 19th and 30th Regiments of Foot, elite units of regulars. Beside them were posted the regulars of the 3rd Regiment, the Buffs.

In the middle, on the road, were provincial regulars which had been evacuated from Ninety-Six: soldiers of the New York Volunteers, the New Jersey Volunteers, and DeLancy's Brigade all under the command of Lt. Col. John Cruger.

On the left of the British line were the British regulars of the battle-tested 63rd and 64th Regiments of Foot. On the far left, Stewart placed his reserves, and mounted under the command of Major John Coffin (Lt. Col. Stewart's report to Lord Cornwallis in Lee, 1812).

Believing he was greatly outnumbered, Lt. Col. Stewart ordered Major Sheridan of the New York Volunteers to retreat to the brick house and hold it if it were necessary to retire from the battle line to the cleared field. It would become necessary (Stewart in Lee, 1812).

Major General Greene lost no time in posting his forces. The columns had been marching in the order Greene intended them to take the field so little time was lost in forming the lines for the battle.

Greene used the same battle plan which had served Brigadier General Daniel Morgan so well at Cowpens but had not been successful at Guilford Courthouse. He posted his militia in the front line. In the middle of the road was the North Carolina militia commanded by Col. Malmedy, a French cavalry officer who had performed poorly at the defense of Charleston (Borick, 2003). Also, he was not well known to the men he commanded whereas all the other officers on the field were well acquainted with the units they commanded.

To the right of the road, and facing the British regulars of the 63rd and 64th Regiments, was Marion's Brigade. Brigadier General Marion and his brigade had campaigned in the swamps and flood plains of the Carolina rivers for over a year. They knew the terrain and the enemy.

To the left of the road and Malmedy's force was the North and South Carolina militia commanded by Brigadier General Andrew Pickens. Pickens had commanded the militia line at Cowpens and was a patriot with great experience and ability. Many of the troops he commanded this day had fought with him before. Others, those of Thomas Sumter's militia, might be new to this commander but they were not new to battle. They had fought British regulars with some success and Greene could be confident of their ability. In addition to command of his brigade, Francis Marion was in command of the first line of militia (Maj. Gen. Nathanael Greene to Washington in Lee, 1812).

The second line consisted of three small brigades of Continentals: North Carolinians, Marylanders and Virginians. General Jethro Sumner's three battalions of North Carolinians were commanded by Lieutenant Colonel Ash, and Majors Armstrong and Blount. They were posted on the right of the line behind Marion's Brigade.

In the center, and behind the North Carolina militia, were the two battalions of Lieutenant Colonel Campbell's Virginians, Major Snead and Captain Edmunds commanding.

Two battalions of Marylanders were posted on the left behind Pickens' militia.

The Maryland troops were under the command of Colonel Otho Holland Williams, who had served in the south during the entire campaign. He had fought at Camden, Guilford Courthouse, Hobkirk's Hill, Ninety-Six and now at Eutaw Springs. One Maryland battalion was commanded by Lieutenant Colonel John Eager Howard, an experienced officer who had commanded the Continental infantry with great success at the Battle of Cowpens (Babits, 1998). The other Maryland battalion was commanded by Major Hardman.

Lee's Legion, infantry and cavalry, commanded by Lieutenant Colonel Henry Lee was posted on the right flank. The left flank was covered by State Troops commanded by Lieutenant Colonel Henderson with Lieutenant Colonels Hampton, Middleton and Polk.

Lieutenant Colonel William Washington's cavalry and Captain Kirkwood's Delaware troops were held in reserve (Major General Greene's report to General George Washington in Lee, 1812).

The artillery consisted of two three-pounders under Captain Lieutenant Gaines, which advanced with the first line and two six-pounders under Captain Browne which advanced with the second line (Greene's report in Lee, 1812).

Lee's Legion and Henderson's State troops had led the advance and it was that party which Major Coffin had attacked. Now the alerted British commander had formed his troops and the American line moved into place.

James describes the situation.

> The effective force of each army was nearly equal, except for cavalry, in which Greene would have had the advantage, if the nature of the ground had permitted the use of it. For none of the ground was then open, and particularly on his left it was scrubby oak (James, 1821:133).

It was in this scrubby oak where Major John Marjoribanks was posted with his elite troops.

Greene's account reports that the firing began with volleys from right to left along his line. This would suggest that Marion's Brigade initiated the action. Where the battle began is a matter of dispute. Although many historians indicate that the British line was a few hundred yards in front of the cleared land, James reports that

> ... the action commenced about a mile from the fountain. Marion and Pickens continued to advance and fire, but the North Carolina militia broke at the third round. Sumner with the new raised troops, then occupied their place and behaved gallantly. Marion's marksmen firing with great precision, and galling the enemy greatly, had now advanced more than half a mile, when the British charged with fixed bayonets, and Marion ordered a retreat (James, 1821:134).

James reports that as Marion cleared the field the Virginians charged the British with bayonets and drove them back. As Marion rallied his men there was a loud huzzah for the Americans which "told the issue of the contest" (James, 1821:134).

Here it is well to remember Norman Mailer's comment that history can never be factual as even participants in an event view the action from their own perspective. It is certainly true here that the combatants on the right of the American line thought that the battle was over and the Americans had taken the field. Although James' account adds the events which later thwarted the American advance, the American huzzahs at this point in his narrative suggest victory.

Although things had gone extremely well on the American right, the left of the American line was not as fortunate. As the Americans moved forward they came under oblique fire from the left where Marjoribanks and his elite troops were posted in the thicket. As commanded, Lt. Col. William Washington charged with his Virginia cavalry. Upon finding that the horses could not penetrate the thicket, Washington changed his order to attempt to force his way around Marjoribanks' position. This maneuver meant that the officers were exposed to the fire from the thicket and all but two of the Virginia officers were killed or wounded in this attempt.

Washington was wounded and pinned under his dead horse and received a bayonet wound in the chest as he lay helpless. Sergeant Major Perry, who is credited with saving Washington's life at Cowpens, fought furiously and was wounded five times (Haller, 2001). Finally, a British officer took Washington prisoner and those who were able left the field (Haller, 2001).

A troop of Lee's cavalry commanded by Eggleston went to assist Washington's troop. Kirkwood's Delaware infantry attacked the thicket and drove Marjoribanks, with his prisoners, back toward the British line. The Delaware Continentals attacked the Buffs with bayonets and the fighting was so severe that Lee comments that men were, in death, impaled on each other's bayonets (Lee, 1812). Others reported wading through ankle-deep puddles of blood.

With the left of the British line driven in, Major Sheridan had retreated from the middle of the British line into the brick house, a contingency which Stewart had suggested before the battle. Closely pursued by Lee's infantry there was a struggle at the door and it was finally closed leaving some soldiers of the New York Volunteers outside the door. Taking them prisoners, and using them as shields, Lee's men retreated. Now, with Sheridan's troops in the safety of the house and Marjoribanks' men in the stockaded garden behind, Stewart attempted to rally his troops.

Greene ordered Lee's cavalry to attack but it was then that Lee realized that Eggleston's troop was not available. Lee maintains that, had his full complement been on the attack, he would have destroyed the British army (Lee, 1812). James reports "Thus a most favourable opportunity of completing the route(sic) already commenced, was irretrievably lost." (James, 1821:135).

The British rout James and others describe occurred on the American right. Camp followers and auxiliary personnel in the British camp, believing all was lost, retreated down the Charleston road after setting fire to equipment and supplies. The panic spread clear to Charleston and slaves there were moved to cut timber across the road near the city. Residents of Charleston believed the Americans were in close pursuit of those who had fled the field at Eutaw Springs.

On the field, American soldiers on the right believed that the battle was over. As they pushed the enemy from the still standing tents of the British camp, they stopped to enjoy the spoils of war. The tents had food and drink, equipment, clothes and shoes. The Americans had been on half-rations and had been marching since four in the morning. Greene reported that they were half-naked and used Spanish moss to prevent their cartridges boxes from rubbing raw skin and to cushion their shoulders against the recoil of their weapons.

The riches of the British camp were irresistible and the men stopped. Officers who were pursuing the enemy, and attempting an attack against the brick house, found that their men were not following them. Also, the looters were being fired upon from the barricaded house and garden.

> Greene now brought up his artillery against the brick house, and sent for Marion who came to his assistance; but the weight of his

> metal was too light to affect a breach. Here, after losing many men and making unavailable efforts he was obliged to desist, bringing off one field piece, which he had taken from the enemy, and losing two of his own. Thus Sheridan and Marjoribanks saved the British army (James, 1821:135).

However, Marjoribanks' bravery had cost dearly as he was mortally wounded in his last attack.

> General Greene, in this manner disappointed in the more sanguine expectation of a complete victory, collected all his wounded, except those under the fire of the enemy, and placing a strong picket on the field of battle, retired sullenly from the ground in search of water. (James, 1821:135-136)

James describes the day as hot and the lack of water serious. In addition to the long march to the battle, the men had fought for three or four hours. The first of the battle was fought in the woods but as the British were pressed back to the clearing, the lack of shade made the need for water intense. Marjoribank's men were in the pallisaded garden just above the springs so Greene's men had no approach to the source of the freshest water in the area.

As they moved back from the battlefield, men drank from the first pond they encountered, a pond where horses and men had traveled through earlier in the day. So desperate with thirst men crawled over others into the pond. James speculates why Greene did not move to the creek as the desire to keep his troops concentrated. James remarks: "It was not from dread of the enemy." (James, 1812:136f)

Later historians would challenge Greene's decision to leave the battle. There were outbuildings which could have been used for protection. There was a possibility of burning the British out of the brick house as had been done at Fort Motte. It is easy to speculate in hindsight, but the men who fought that day did not dispute the wisdom of Greene's decision. It was evident that the British army was not going to elude them and they could, and would, return the next day intending to finish the job.

CHAPTER VIII

THE AFTERMATH

Why did Greene retreat from the battlefield at Eutaw Springs?

First, most accounts refer to the necessity of water. As the day progressed and the temperature rose, there was increasing danger of heat stroke. Greene had always been mindful of that possibility as evidenced by the fact that he confined his training and marching to early and/or late hours to escape the midday heat.

Second, and possibly the most urgent, was the need to reorganize in the face of serious losses. Lt. Col. William Washington was a prisoner and most of his officers were killed or wounded.

The commander of the Virginians, Col. Campbell, was dead. Of the remaining Continental officers, only Williams and Lee were unhurt.

Militia General Andrew Pickens had been carried off the field after being shot in the chest. His followers believed the shot had been fatal but, fortunately, the bullet had struck the buckle of his sword belt and driven it into his breast bone. The wound, although serious, had not been fatal but the impact had rendered him unconscious.

In a private letter to Eli Williams of Washington Country,

Maryland, on 11 September, Colonel Otho Williams writes: "Lt. Col. Washington, and Lt. McGuire and 27 others were wounded and imprisoned, and a great number now sleep in that Great Bed of Honor." (Gibbes, III, 1853)

Later, in an official report, Colonel Otho Williams listed the casualties:

Of the Maryland Brigade. Killed: Captain Dobson; Captain Edgerly; Lieutenant Dewall; Lieutenant Gould. Wounded: Lieutenant Colonel Howard; Captain Gibson; Captain Lieutenant Hugon; Lieutenant Ewing; Lieutenant Woolford; Lieutenant Lynn; Ensign Moore.

Of the Virginia Brigade. Killed: Lieutenant Colonel Campbell; Captain Oldham; Lieutenant Wilson. Wounded: Captain Edmonds; Captain Morgan; Lieutenant Miller; Lieutenant Jonitt.

North Carolina Brigade. Killed: Captain William Goodman; Captain Christopher Goodwin; Captain Dennis Porterfield; Lieutenant John Dillon. Wounded: Captain Joshua Hadley; Lieutenant Charles Dixon; Lieutenant Richard Andrews; Lieutenant Thomas Dudley; Ensign Abner Lamb; Ensign James Moore.(See Endnote 7)

South Carolina Line. Wounded: Lieutenant Colonel Henderson.

Cavalry: Lieutenant Colonel William Washington, wounded and a prisoner of the British. Killed: Captain Watts; Lieutenant Gordon*; Lieutenant Simons*; Lieutenant King*; Steward, Mr. Carlisle, volunteer. (*See Endnote 8).

Artillery. Wounded: Captain Finn; Lieutenant Carson (mortally); Lieutenant Drew; Lieutenant M'Gurrie (Also a prisoner of war.)

Legion Infantry. Wounded: Lieutenant Manning; Mr. Carrington, volunteer.

The report obviously refers to the Continental units. (Williams in Gibbes III, 1853).

The following are militia and state troops casualties.
South Carolina State Officers. Killed: Major Rutherford; Lieutenant Polk; Adjutant Lush (Lusk?). Wounded: Lieutenant Colonel Henderson (also on the above list); Lieutenant Colonel Middleton; Captain Moore; Captain Giles; Captain N. Martin; Captain Cowan; Lieutenant Erskine; Lieutenant Culpepper; Lieutenant Hammond; Lieutenant Spragins.
South Carolina Militia. Killed: Lieutenant Holmes; Lieutenant Simons**. Wounded: Brigadier General Andrew Pickens; Lieutenant Colonel Horry**; Captain Gee; Captain Pegee; Lieutenant Boon.(**See Endnote 9)

Greene moved his army back to Burdell's where they had camped the previous night. It must have been a morose scene as they dealt with the scores of wounded. Those who had survived the battle were in danger of succumbing to the many fevers and infections which were rampant in the close quarters of camp life.

Greene wrote an order the following morning expressing his thanks to the officers and soldiers of the army and commending the commanders for their "extraordinary exertions in the well fought battle of yesterday."

> The very great advantage of a strong brick house, was the strong hold of preserving the remains of the British army from captivity; and though the want of water made it requisite, after the action, to retire to this place, yet the victory is complete, and we have only to lament the loss of several of our brave officers and soldiers, whose glorious deaths are to be envied.
> (Greene, 1997:307)

Although he had left the field, Major General Greene had

no intention of allowing the British to remain unchallenged at Eutaw Springs. On the morning of the 9th he ordered Lee's Legion and Marion's Brigade to move around the British and secure the road along which the British must retreat and the reenforcements for Stewart from Monck's Corner were marching (Lee, 1812). This area was where Marion's plantation stood and where he and many of his militiamen had traveled. The trails through the swamps were known to Marion and he moved easily through the area. The troops intended to take a posting at Ferguson's swamp on the road between Eutaw Springs and Monck's Corner.

At Burdell's Plantation Greene prepared to move again to Eutaw Springs. He had intended to challenge the British who remained but the weather was rainy and would make firing the weapons difficult. Now he decided to watch and wait.

Meanwhile, at the British camp at Eutaw Springs preparations were being made to abandoned the area. The American troops, a strong picket commanded by Lieutenant Colonel Wade Hampton, watched as the British collected the weapons of the dead and wounded, stacked them and set them afire. Supplies of rum were poured into the springs.

It was here at Eutaw Springs, on 9 September, that Lt. Col. Stewart wrote his report to Lord Cornwallis. He gave his account of the battle and wrote:

> I hope, my lord, when it is considered that such a handful of men, attacked by the united force of Generals Greene, Sumter, Marion, Sumner and Pickens, and the Legions of Colonels Lee and Washington, driving them from the field of battle, and taking the only two six-pounders they had, deserve some merit.....I hope your lordship will excuse any inaccuracy that may be in this letter, as I have been a good deal indisposed by a wound I

received in my left elbow, which, though slight, from its situation is troublesome. (Stewart in Lee, 1812:605)

The report included those killed as 3 officers, 6 sergeants and 76 rank and file. Wounded were 16 officers, 20 sergeants and 315 rank and file. Those numbers may be accurate but those listed as missing, 10 officers, 15 sergeants, and 232 rank and file, must be greatly underestimated as the Americans had held more prisoners than that even before Stewart abandoned his seriously wounded soldiers on the field as he retreated. A history of the 64th Regiment of Foot (Urwin, nd) gives the same numbers of killed and wounded but indicates that 430 were missing.

Lt. Col. Stewart, in the same report, had complained of his lack of intelligence and had greatly overestimated the numbers Major General Greene had at his disposal. Actually the numbers engaged on each side were approximately equal although Stewart reported that his army was "much reduced by sickness and otherwise." Thus, it is not surprising that he listed General Sumter as present at the battle although Sumter had not been with Greene's army for some time.

On the evening of 9 September Stewart gave up the field at Eutaw Springs. Much materiel would be destroyed as the British did not have the means of carrying it all off. The British did not take time to bury their dead but left them on the field along with over seventy British soldiers who were too severely wounded to be moved. In addition a few American wounded were left on the field if they were too seriously wounded to travel as prisoners. Marching British troops were strung out along the road to Monck's Corner.

When the burning weapons and ammunition started to explode, the retreating columns thought they were under attack and some teamsters cut their horses out of the wagon harness and rode the horses toward Charleston in panic.

Stores were being burned all along the road as the British attempted to destroy anything which could be of use to the American army. Trees were felled across the road in hopes of hindering the progress of the American army.

Lee and Marion were below Eutaw Springs intent on preventing the British retreat. However, their intelligence indicated that Major McArthur and his reinforcements were approaching and would soon meet Stewart's retreating army. Rather than be caught between two large British forces, Lee and Marion moved back to report to Major General Greene (Lee, 1812). As James reports "To fight between two fires, became hazardous, and the junction of the enemy was effected." (James 1821:136). However, the British rear guard was constantly under attack and Lee and Marion took prisoners of stragglers.

The events had few characteristics of a British victory as Stewart hurriedly moved his troops and the American army followed. Stewart stopped at Martin's Tavern near Ferguson Swamp and was met there by Major McArthur on the morning of 10 September and the combined army moved toward Monck's Corner which Lee reckoned to be about one day's march from Charleston.

Greene's army followed the British down the road toward Monck's Corner as Lee and Marion continued to harass the British columns taking prisoners. At one point they captured wagons carrying the wounded and, after removing the American wounded prisoners, released the wagons to continue their trek toward Charleston (Lee, 1812).

Major General Greene with his army arrived at Ferguson's Swamp too late to engage the retreating British army. On 11 September he wrote his report to General George Washington from his headquarters at Martin's Tavern near Ferguson's Swamp. His account has been used as a basis for this work and is widely available. (Lee, 1812:600-603).

With no hope of engaging the British before they reached

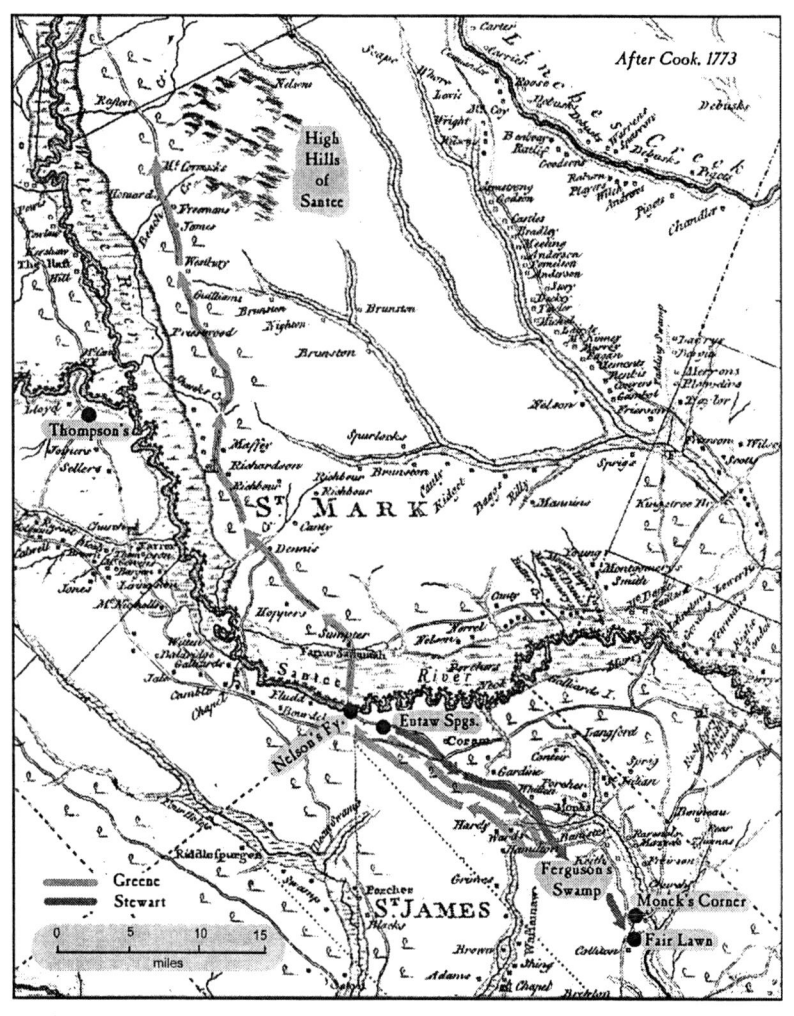

Stewart retreated into Ferguson's Swamp followed by Greene. Greene returned to Eutaw Springs, picked up his wounded, crossed at Nelson's Ferry, and returned to High Hills of Santee.

Charleston, Greene returned to the battlefield at Eutaw Springs. Burying the dead and gathering up the wounded of his own army and those of the enemy left by Stewart, he moved to Nelson's Ferry and crossed the Santee River. He moved north to the High Hills of the Santee where he would once again encamp. Here he would rest his suffering army and tend to the needs of the wounded.

Lee reports that when the army arrived at the High Hills on 19 September that

> ..disease had resumed its wasting havoc, brought on by the forty-eight hours' hard service; throughout which we were exposed to the sultry sun during the day, and to the heavy dew during the night. Never had we experienced so much sickness at any one time as we did now; nor was it confined to new levies, as was customary, but affected every corps; even those inured to military life, and most accustomed to the climate (Lee, 1812:477).

However,

> Marion and his militia, being habituated to the swamps of the Pedee, were less affected by the prevailing fever, and continued on the south of the Congaree, to protect the country from the predatory excursions of the enemy" (Lee, 1812:477).

Lee's observation may have been partly correct as to the resistance of Marion and his men, but if crowding and contagion were part of the problem, Marion's men would have escaped much of that. Marion did not go into camp with Greene's army but returned to Peyre's Plantation. However, his correspondence with Greene indicates that Marion was ill with a fever although still able to function (Greene, 1997).

After a brief stay, Marion moved upriver from Peyre's Plantation to Cantey's Plantation, another safe haven. Now, when Greene's army was encamped at the High Hills, Marion sought the isolation of Cantey's Plantation.

Not only was Greene's army suffering, but the British army was in a similar condition. Lt. Col. Stewart had left his seriously wounded along the way and many died. The brave Marjoribanks who had been severely wounded in his last attack was left at a plantation along the road. He died on 22 October, six weeks after the battle.

Death did not come quickly to many of the wounded. James writes of the situation of Greene's army as they camped at the High Hills.

> Many of Greene's wounded officers and men died and lie buried on a hill......No mound or grave stone points out the spot where such brave men repose. Even the mounds, where the dead at Eutaw Springs were buried, have been violated by the cutting of a ditch through them. Alas! My country, why have such things been suffered?" (James, 1822:138).

The area which James describes is in the vicinity of the area of Stateburg, South Carolina. Thomas Sumter acquired land and resided here after the war. He is buried there in a marked grave. There are no other cemeteries or grave markers to commemorate the scores of soldiers who died there of wounds suffered at Hobkirk's Hill, Ninety-Six and Eutaw Springs.

As Greene cared for his army at the High Hills, he sent home the North Carolina militia whose terms of enlistments were due to expire. To this group he gave the task of escorting his prisoners to Salisbury, North Carolina.

Thomas Myers reported in his pension application that he had served in the North Carolina Militia for three months in a regiment commanded by Colonel Malbide(sic), a Frenchman.

> ..we were marched down to South Carolina and finally made attack on the British at a place called Eutaw Springs where we killed or wounded about nine hundred of the enemy and took about three hundred prisoners. After the battle, the company I belonged to was dispatched with the prisoners that were taken to be guarded at Salisbury, North Carolina. When we had gone as far as Camden with these prisoners, the commander of the guard, whose name I now forget, calculated he had enough men to guard them without my company. We were about to be sent back to the army where a few more prisoners were taken, As our time was near over, we told our Colonel that if he would give us our discharge we would take those prisoners on to Salisbury and then go home. Accordingly, we went on to Salisbury with the prisoners and then went home. (Myers, 1832).

This report is consistent with Lee's account that after the battle Marion and Lee continued to take prisoners until the final count of prisoners taken was five hundred.

CHAPTER IX

YORKTOWN

Major General Nathanael Greene's army rested at the High Hills. Now, in addition to the many wounded from recent battles, Lee reported more sickness than he had ever seen (Lee, 1812). With the British army moving its forces toward the safety of Charleston, Greene's correspondence reflected a concern about Lord Cornwallis. In a letter to Marion he suggests that militia needed to be on constant alert in case Lord Cornwallis decided to move again into the south. Marion remained in the field as ordered (Greene, 1997).

Finally, word arrived that the French fleet had moved into the Chesapeake Bay, landed French troops in the area, and then, on 5 September, had defeated the British fleet. Lord Cornwallis, encamped at Yorktown, was without the support of the British navy which had retreated to New York Harbor to be repaired and refitted. Lord Cornwallis had no hope of escape without the return of the British Navy with reinforcements from General Clinton's command in New York City. However, General Clinton, was preoccupied with strengthening his position as he expected an attack against New York by Washington's army.

Nevertheless, Major General Greene, still cautious, watched for any sign that Lord Cornwallis would try to break out of his position in Virginia and return to the south. Soon word was received that General George Washington had moved, not to New York as the British had expected, but to Virginia. Here the American forces under Washington joined with French troops commanded by Compte de Rochambeau to attack Lord Cornwallis at Yorktown.

The American and French forces began the siege on 28 September 1781, just 20 days after the Battle of Eutaw Springs. Lord Cornwallis' correspondence indicates that he had been assured of reinforcements by Clinton. Those reinforcements did not arrive until it was too late. Lord Cornwallis was forced to surrender his 9,000 troops on 19 October 1781. Clinton's relief force arrived by ship a week later and, seeing that the battle had already been lost, turned and headed back to New York.

In the minds of many Americans, the British defeat at Yorktown ended the War of American Independence but that is not the case. Yorktown ended Lord Cornwallis' attempt to win the war by winning the Southern Campaign but it did not end the war.

In South Carolina Major General Greene petitioned General Washington for troops (Greene, 1997). Greene hoped that the French fleet could bombard Charleston while he attacked by land. With Charleston and then Savannah taken, the British presence in the south would be abolished. A few troops were sent, but the French fleet moved back to the Carribean where it was defeated in an encounter with the British Navy.

What had to be done in Carolina would have to be accomplished by Greene with little help from outside the area. Again he ordered militia into the field to oppose the Tories and prevent the British from moving out of Charleston Neck. On 18 November the camp at the High

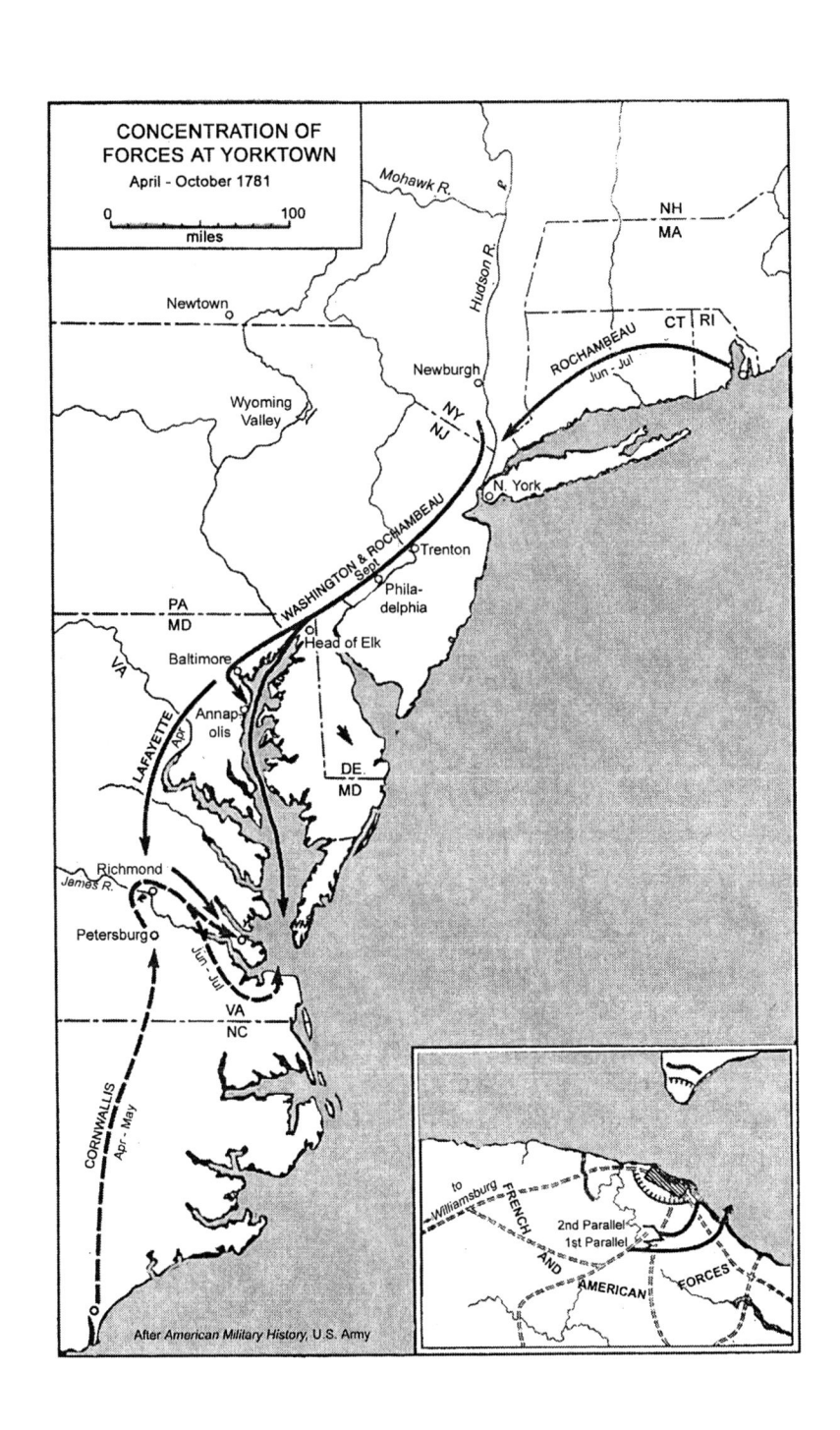

CONCENTRATION OF FORCES AT YORKTOWN
April – October 1781

0 — 100 miles

Mohawk R.
Hudson R.
NH / MA
Newtown
Newburgh
Wyoming Valley
ROCHAMBEAU
Jun - Jul
CT / RI
NY / NJ
N. York
WASHINGTON & ROCHAMBEAU
Sept
Trenton
Philadelphia
PA / MD
Baltimore
Head of Elk
VA
Annapolis
DE / MD
LAFAYETTE
Apr
Richmond
James R.
Petersburg
Jun - Jul
VA / NC
CORNWALLIS
Apr - May

to Williamsburg
2nd Parallel
1st Parallel
FRENCH AND AMERICAN FORCES

After *American Military History*, U.S. Army

Hills was abandoned and Greene moved his forces into the low country where he could better feed his troops and reoccupy as much of the area as possible. British forces still were posted at Goose Creek and Dorchester but were moving toward Charleston.

Word of the defeat at Yorktown arrived in England on 25 November 1781 (Cook, 1995). The populous was shocked as they remembered Lord Cornwallis' great victories at Camden and Guilford Courthouse. Many did not understand the importance of the British losses at King's Mountain, Cowpens and the many skirmishes in the back country. Nor was it widely understood that, even though victorious, Lord Cornwallis had suffered 25% casualties at Camden (Pancake, 1985), and another 27% at Guilford Courthouse (Hairr, 2002).

However, with the loss of Lord Cornwallis's troops at Yorktown, and the failure of that campaign to conquer the south, the Prime Minister, Lord North, knew that any further effort to defeat the colonists was futile. However, the King and Lord Germaine insisted that the war could still be won.

General Clinton held New York City and harbor, British forces held Canada, Rhode Island and the ports of Wilmington, Charleston and Savannah. General Clinton's force in New York numbered over 17,000 (Stokesbury,1991) and there were still 8,000 effectives (British troops able to fight) in Charleston. The British Navy had redeemed itself by defeating the French fleet in the islands and was once again a significant force. With the King resolute in his determination not to lose the colonies, and Lord Germaine still a powerful force in the government, the war continued.

In the months after Yorktown Lord North tried repeatedly to resign and to force the formation of a new government from the opposition whose agenda was to end the war. The King refused to meet with the leaders of the opposition party and Lord Germaine stymied Lord North's efforts, so the war continued. It was not until March of 1782 that Lord North, facing a vote of "no confidence," resigned and the opposition party formed a government and started the process which would eventually end the war. One of the first acts was to replace General Clinton with General Guy Carleton.

Although General Carleton's role would be to disengage the British Army and to conclude the war (Cook, 1995), he did not arrive in America until May of 1782. It would take a full eighteen months from the time he arrived until the British finally departed from New York (Cook, 1995).

Although General Carleton was to inform the Americans of his orders, the American commanders were not immediately aware of this. Nor were Tory militia, especially in the south. Some, still believing that England would eventually win the war, and others, determined to punish their neighbors for past wrongs (and there were many), still campaigned.

Nowhere was the brutality of the engagements more severe than in the south. General Greene's correspondence reflects his concern for the savagery of the participants on both sides. Especially heinous to Greene were the murders of prisoners such as had occurred at Augusta's Fort Grierson by the Georgia militia. Although deplorable, Lee writes that it was understandable since the Georgians had suffered brutal treatment from British and Tory alike (Lee, 1812).

In South Carolina Tory militia commanded by Col. William "Bloody Bill" Cunningham attacked and murdered surrendered prisoners at Clouds Creek on 17 November 1781. Among those killed were Col. Butler and one of his sons (Lumpkin, 1981).

Two days later Cunningham attacked Hayes Station and burned out the defenders. After Colonel Hayes (See Endnote 10) surrendered, Cunningham personally killed Hayes and 14 of the captured men (Lumpkin, 1981).

In May Cunningham' militia was surprised in the Saluda

River area by Captain William Butler, son and brother of the Clouds Creek massacre victims (Lambert, 1987). Although Cunningham escaped on an unsaddled horse, his unit was decimated. (See Endnote 11).

With the interior of South Carolina under American control, Governor Rutledge established a seat of government at Jacksonboro, just 30 miles from the British stronghold in Charleston. The government formed included Francis Marion and Thomas Sumter as senators and Andrew Pickens as a representative.

Still, General Greene depended on the militia commanded by Marion to maintain control of the area and to prevent the British from sending troops out of Charleston to capture cattle and crops.

Governor Rutledge often required Marion to be at Jacksonboro in order to make a quorum, and at other times, required him to move Tory families from their plantations toward Charleston. The rationale was that these families had supported the British, now let the British support them. The demands of the governor required Marion to be absent from his command and this presented a problem for General Greene's agenda.

Although the militia were required to serve for 30 days a year, many of Marion's Brigade had greatly exceeded that. However, they fought when, where and for whom they chose. Some commanders who now rode with Marion's Brigade did not elicit the same loyalty as Marion and the brigade seems to have been less effective when Marion did not personally command. Even when he returned to command in a skirmish, the brigade was not as effective as it had been when he commanded full-time.

The British, now confined to Charleston Neck and a few of the nearby islands, never attempted a full-scale attack on Greene's army. However, detachments were dispatched from Charleston to capture beef and produce in the area surrounding Charleston. In August 1782, at Fair Lawn, British forces broke through Marion's line and forced him to retreat. Although Marion retreated in good order it was his last engagement of the war.

The action was not confined to the low country around Charleston. In November, a Loyalist commander, Thomas Waters, led the Cherokees in raids against the frontier settlements. Brigadier General Andrew Pickens of South Carolina and Lt. Col. Elijah Clarke of Georgia led an expedition of 414 men against the Cherokees. Waters escaped but the Indian villages were attacked and burned. On 17 October 1782, a year after Cornwallis surrendered his army at Yorktown, the Indian chiefs signed a peace treaty ending the Cherokee Wars.

As peace talks continued, the noose around Charleston tightened. General Leslie, the British commander, arranged for an evacuation of Charleston on 14 December 1782, fifteen months after the Battle of Yorktown. Savannah had been evacuated the previous July. There was considerable difficulty in evacuating Charleston due to the numbers requiring transportation. Finally, three hundred ships accomplished the transportation of forty-two hundred Loyalists and their slaves and household goods as well as the British regulars and provincials who were posted in Charleston (Edgar, 1998).

Units of British regulars and many civilians and slaves were transported to Jamaica. Later, the British soldiers were returned to Great Britain. Many of the Loyalists stayed in the islands and established businesses there. Some Loyalists were transported directly to Halifax, Nova Scotia.

Units of provincial soldiers who had been enlisted from New York, New Jersey and surrounding areas were returned by ship to New York. In the next year, many would sail from Paulus Hook to Nova Scotia, Canada, and start a new life there (Lambert, 1987).

As the British withdrew, the Continental Army took control of the city. However, the militia which had accompanied it on the march through South Carolina was conspicuously absent. They were forbidden to enter Charleston even as spectators. Francis Marion, who had no interest in entering the city which he thought unhealthy, had dismissed his troops and returned to his home.

Major General Nathanael Greene was hailed as a hero. Rightly so. He had broken the British hold on the south and, unlike Cornwallis who lost his Southern Campaign, Greene had won his.

When Nathanael Greene made his decision after the battle of Guilford Courthouse to take back the occupied territory in the Carolinas and Georgia, he had one goal in mind. He would deny England an opportunity to claim and keep land which Cornwallis had thought was securely in British hands. It is possible that without this successful campaign England would have claimed North Carolina, South Carolina and Georgia and, instead of thirteen colonies, the new nation would have been reduced to ten.

In a series of encounters with the British, Greene had been frustrated at every turn. However, his strategy was sound and, when the hostilities were over, he had won back the south. The cost had been great. Never more so than at Eutaw Springs but General George Washington's confidence in Nathanael Greene had been justified.

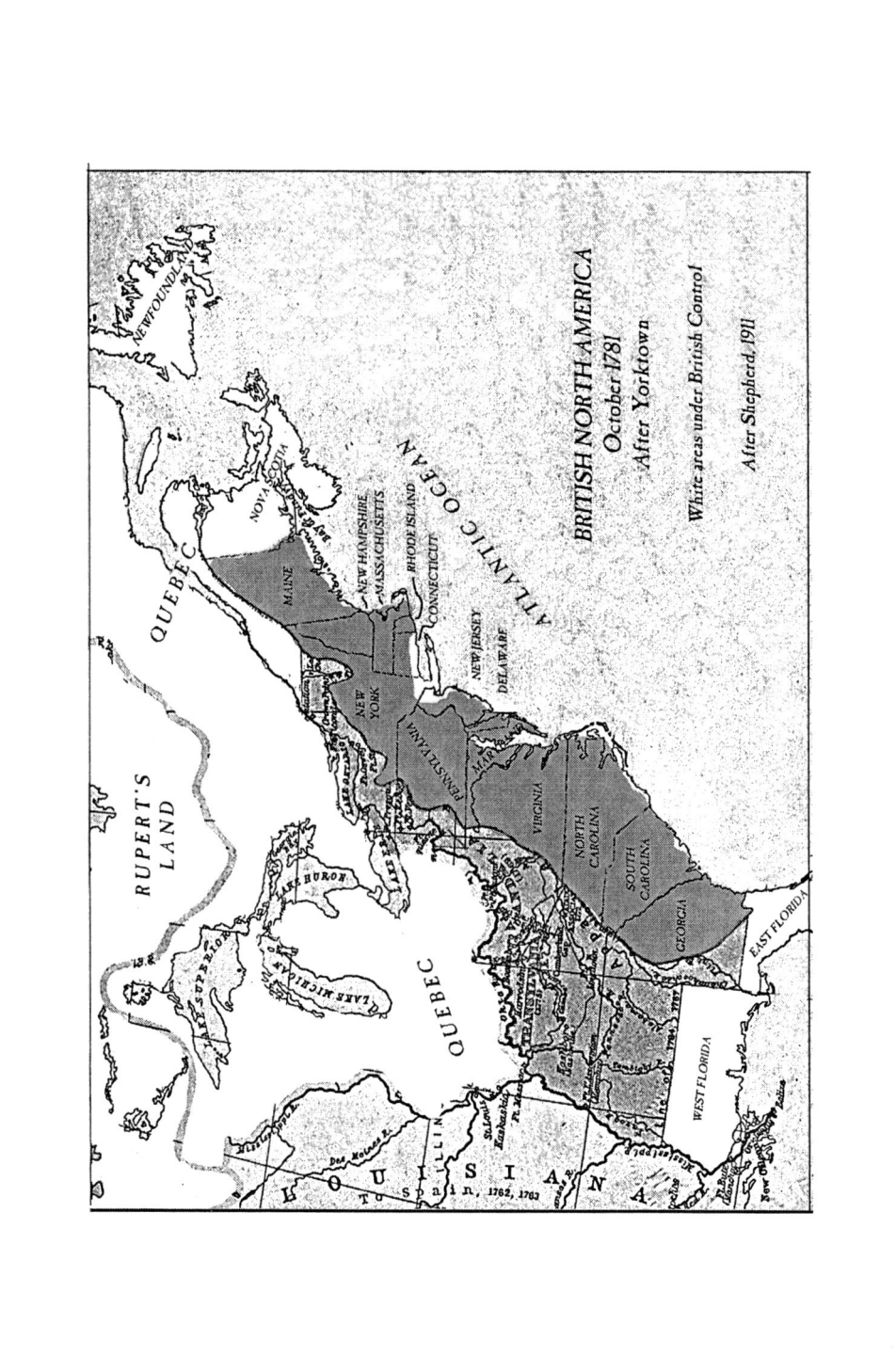

BRITISH NORTH AMERICA
October 1781
After Yorktown

White areas under British Control

After Shepherd, 1911

CHAPTER X

WHO WON AT EUTAW SPRINGS?

Modern historians remark that Nathanael Greene never won a battle. Perhaps that has colored their interpretation of what happened at Eutaw Springs. Certainly the British are credited with a win by most historians although a few suggest it was a draw.

On what basis should we decide?

Alexander Stewart, in his report written to Lord Cornwallis on 9 September 1781, while he was still at the battle site, states unequivocally that he had won the battle. Did he overstate his case?

In his report (Stewart to Cornwallis in Lee, 1812) Stewart under-reported the number of men missing. Even if the numbers he reported killed and wounded were accurate, it would have been a pyrrhic victory like Cornwallis had suffered at Guilford Courthouse. But at Guilford Courthouse Cornwallis had clearly held the field. Did Stewart hold the field at Eutaw Springs? And how much of the field must one hold in order to make that claim?

James maintains that the British line was situated about a mile from the springs (James, 1822). O'Kelley places the first skirmish at two miles (O'Kelley, 2005). Others report that the battle line was from two hundred yards to five hundred yards in front of the brick mansion. In any case, there is agreement that the engagement of the first lines occurred in the woods and not in the present memorial park of a few acres. James reports that Marion's men advanced a half a mile before attacked by the bayonets of the 63rd and 64th Regiments of Foot.

The Americans on the right of the line cleared the field and then ransacked the British camp which was astride the road in front of the brick house. There is little doubt that the Americans were pushed back from the British camp by Major Coffin, that the brick house was held by the New York Volunteers, and the pallisaded garden adjoining the house to the rear was claimed by Major Marjoribanks. James reports that Coffin and Marjoribanks had saved the whole British army from destruction.

When Greene retired from the field he left a strong picket under the command of Wade Hampton. How much of the field did Hampton control? Certainly these are questions to be answered by an in-depth study of the field, but a few questions will be addressed here.

Stewart left over seventy wounded British soldiers on the field as well as wounded Americans. He did not leave all the wounded behind has Lee reports overtaking wagons of wounded as the British moved towards Charleston (Lee, 1812). Is it possible that the British did not control enough of the field of battle to recover all of their wounded?

And the British dead were left unburied. At Cowpens, Morgan left the patriot militia to bury the dead on that field and over one hundred and fifty were buried in about twenty-four hours. Why did Stewart leave his dead unburied? Is it possible that he did not control enough of the field to recover them? Certainly those who died in the woods would have been beyond his reach. If the battle had been over by about noon, and Stewart was still on the battle field the next day, why were the dead and wounded unattended?

Although later historians insist that the British won or at best, the Americans had managed a draw, the reports of the battle at that time were quite different.

Greene reported:

> The very great advantage of a strong brick house, was the strong hold of preserving the remains of the British army from captivity; and though the want of water made it requisite, after the action, to retire to this place, yet the victory is complete, and we have only to lament the loss of several of our brave officers and soldiers, whose glorious deaths are to be envied. Greene's General Orders, Burdle's (sic), September 9, 1781. (Greene, 1997:307).

To Washington, Greene wrote:

> Since I wrote you, we have had the most bloody battle. It was, by far, the most obstinate fight I ever saw. Victory was ours; and had it not been for one of those little incidents which often occur in the progress of war, we should have taken the whole British army. Nothing could exceed the gallantry of our officers, or the bravery of our troops. (Johnson, 1822 :240).

On 11 September 1781 Greene wrote a report to Congress from Martin's Tavern near Ferguson's Swamp which was on the road to Monck's Corner and below Eutaw Springs.

> We have taken 500 Prisoners, including the Wounded the Enemy left behind; and I cannot think they have suffered less than 600 more in killed and Wounded. The fugitives that fled from the field of Battle spread such an alarm that the Enemy burnt their Stores at Dorchester, and abandoned the Post at Fair Lawn, and a great number of Negroes and others were employed in falling Trees across the Road for some Miles without the Gates of Charles Town. Nothing but the brick House, and the particular strength of the position at Eutaw saved the remains of the British Army from being all made Prisoners. I think myself principally indebted for the victory we obtained to the free use of the Bayonet made by the Virginians and Marylanders, the Infantry of the Legion, and Captain Kirkwoods Light Infantry and tho' few Armies ever exhibited equal bravery with ours in general, yet the conduct and intrepidity of these Corps were peculiarly conspicuous. (Greene, 1997: 332).

To General Varnum, a friend and a member of Congress, Greene wrote:

> I have the pleasure to inform you, that we have had a most tremendous fight, and gained a victory. You will see my letter to congress, and have an opportunity to converse with Captain Pierce, my aid (sic), who will have the honour of deliverying you this letter; therefore, I will not go into particulars, but depend on it, it was by far the

most obstinate fight I ever saw. (Greene in Johnson, 1822:239).

And to another friend Greene wrote:

> We have had a most bloody battle since I wrote you before. It was fought at the Eutaw Springs near Nelson's Ferry. We obtained a complete victory and had it not been for one of those incidents to which military operations are subject, we should have taken the whole British army. However, we took five hundred prisoners, and killed and wounded a much greater number, and have driven the enemy almost to the gates of Charleston; we also took near one thousand stand of arms. It was, by far, the hottest action I ever saw, and the most bloody for the numbers engaged . (Greene in Johnson, 1822: 239).

Greene was not alone in his opinion. Col. Otho Wlliams, who, as adjutant-general was second in command on the battlefield, wrote on September 11, 1781:

> Victory is ours, after one of the bloodiest battles ever fought in America; Gen. Greene was determined to drive the enemy from the Up Country; he drove Lt. Col. Stewart as far as Eutaw; Greene led his forces into action on the morning of September 8, and met the enemy about four miles from this camp; our (the American) vivacity equalled the obstinacy of the enemy, and ultimately the Enemy were defeated and obliged to retire to

their Camp; a big brick house there offered refuge to many of them; about five hundred prisoners, including 20 officers, were taken, and the number of wounded is not yet certain.....Greene has followed the enemy more than 20 miles, forcing them to give up a strong position about four miles from here, through they had had reinforcements of 300 or 400 men; the enemy is now at Monks Corner, about 30 miles from Charles Town; hopes soon to be able to take a much-needed post of ease. (Williams in Gibbes, Vol. I: 115-116).

Williams wrote again on 15 October 1781:

Since the Glorious Victory which our Little Army obtain'd over the British at Eutaw, both sides have enough to do in taking care of their sick and wounded; this is the season of epidemic fevers in this climate; all of the wounded of Maryland are likely to recover save Lieut. (William) Woolford, who must undergo the awful change in a day or two; vastly more lamentable to lose an officer in sick quarters than in the field. (Williams in Gibbes. Vol. I:116).

From the reports from the field, it is obvious that those Americans who were engaged believed that the Americans had won the battle. Also, others who were not present but learning of the encounter thought the Americans won. Governor John Rutledge, who accompanied Greene's troops as far as Burdell's and had stayed behind the lines while the battle was fought, wrote to Francis Marion on 15 September 1781 with orders. His opening was:

> I think after the glorious victory at Eutaw...(Gibbs,III,1853:162).

General George Washington replied to Greene's account as he camped before Yorktown on 6 October 1781:

> How happy I am, my dear sir, in at length having it in my power to congratulate you upon a victory, as splendid as I hope it will prove important. Fortune must have been coy indeed, had she not yielded, at last, to so perseverating a person as you have been. I hope now she is yours, she will change her appellation of fickle to that of constant. (Greene, 1997:429).

The Battle at Eutaw Springs did not go unnoticed by Congress:

> By the United States in Congress assembled. October 29th, 1781.
>
> Resolved. That the thanks of the United States in Congress assembled, be presented to Major General Greene, for his wise, decisive, and magnanimous conduct in the action of the 8th of September last, near the Eutaw Springs, in South Carolina; in which, with a force inferior in number to that of the enemy, he obtained a most signal victory........
>
> Resolved. That a British standard be presented to Major-General Greene, as an honorable testimony of his merit, and a

golden medal emblematical of the battle and victory aforesaid......

Resolved. That the thanks of the United States, in Congress assembled, be presented to Brigadier-General Marion, of the South Carolina militia, for his wise, gallant, and decided conduct in defending the liberties of his country; and particularly for his prudent and intrepid attack on a body of British troops, on the 30th day of August last,(See Endnote 12) and for the distinguished part he took in the battle of the 8th of September." (Lee, 1811: 474)

Another interesting reference to the Battle of Eutaw Springs is in a Hessian diary written by a common soldier in an Ansbach-Bayreuth regiment as he was encamped at the siege of Yorktown. He wrote:

> 25 August. A bloody battle took place at Eutaw Springs in South Carolina, between the American forces under General Greene and the British troops under Major General Stewart, in which the English lost four cannon and more than one thousand men. The Americans lost six hundred men and defeated the English. (Dohla, Burgoyne (Translator) 1990: 159).

Obviously the date is wrong as well as the rank of the British commander, Lt. Col. Stewart. A note indicates that Dohla probably wrote entries after the fact. However, it does suggest that a Hessian soldier at Yorktown had heard of the Battle of Eutaw Springs and believed that the British had lost!

Lee's comment of the battle, published in 1811, when it appears that historians had decided the battle was a British victory, is probably close to the mark:

> The honor of the day was claimed by both sides, while the benefits flowing from it were yielded to the Americans; the first belonged to neither, and the last to us. (Lee, 1811:473).

Whether or not Greene won the battle, he had won the campaign. The battle at Eutaw Springs is the culmination of his efforts, and the ground at Eutaw Springs is surely a hallowed spot where "the mould has been moistened by the best blood of our country." (Johnson, 1822:x).

If in this wreck of ruin, they
Can yet be thought to claim a tear,
O smite thy gentle breast, and say
The friends of freedom slumber here.

Philip Freneau

APPENDIX

It is important that we remember who these patriots were who commanded at this historic battle. The men who fought at Eutaw Springs did not sink into oblivion. With the war over, the weary troops returned to their homes, or sought new ones with land grants given for their service. Many were instrumental in rebuilding the shattered countryside. Some became nationally known: others had an impact locally.

PATRIOT FORCES-CONTINENTALS

Major General Nathanael Greene, commander of the patriot forces in the south from late 1780 until the end of the war, left the service after the war ended. In gratitude for his services Georgia made him a gift of a plantation on the Savannah River above Savannah. The Greenes also acquired property on Cumberland Island on the coast of Georgia. Later South Carolina gave him property.

Although Greene attempted to make a living as a planter, he was plagued by creditors for payment for supplies he had procured for his almost naked troops. When the agent involved declared bankruptcy, the creditors demanded payment from Greene. The South Carolina property was sold to pay debts.

Although Greene should not have been personally

responsible for debts accrued in the service of the army, he was preoccupied with attempts to solve this problem. One of the impediments in settling this financial matter was Thomas Sumter who, as a senator in South Carolina, and later as a member of Congress, continued a vendetta against Greene to Greene's death and even to his widow. Greene was long dead before the matter was settled.

Nathanael Greene died in Georgia, on 19 June 1786 and was buried in Savannah. It was reported that he died of heat stroke and, if that were the case, it would be ironic for such a condition to fell a commander who was so careful to protect his army from the effects of heat. Others believe that his health had been impaired by long and exhaustive service in the Southern Campaign and the worry about his debts, and died of a heart attack. In either case it was a premature end of a great soldier and patriot. He had just passed his forty-fourth birthday. At his funeral, the eulogy paid tribute to the enormous powers of his mind. Henry Lee, (Light Horse Harry), now in Congress, chaired a committee which authorized a monument to Greene. It was ninety years before the monument was erected at the intersection of Massachusetts and Maryland Avenues in Washington.

General Jethro Sumner, commander of the North Carolina Continentals at the Battle of Eutaw Springs, was born about 1733. He was a prosperous tavern owner from Warren County, North Carolina, when he joined the service in 1776. The North Carolina troops saw service in the northern theater, and were encamped with Washington's troops at Valley Forge. Sumner became seriously ill and returned to North Carolina to recuperate. Although the officer corp of the North Carolinians was a contentious group due to unacceptable promotion policies, Sumner remained in the service.

The North Carolinians moved from the north to the south during the British campaign against Savannah, then were taken prisoners when Charleston was surrendered to the British. Sumner was not at Charleston but was in North Carolina when his troops were taken and it fell to him to rebuild the North Carolina Continental Line. With Lord Cornwallis just over the North Carolina border in Virginia there was little enthusiasm for service. Also, smallpox outbreaks made it difficult to assemble troops. In spite of the difficulties Sumner assembled a new North Carolina Continental line which fought at Eutaw Springs.

Sumner was plagued with ill health throughout his service and only lived two years after the war. He died about 1785 and was buried in Warren County. Schenck (1889) laments that no memorial was built to honor a man who is believed to be one of the great North Carolina heroes and not even a town in that state was named after him. That appears to have been corrected later as Sumner's body was removed and reburied at Guilford Courthouse. There is now a town of Sumner in Tennessee which would have been western North Carolina during the Revolutionary War.

Colonel Otho Holland Williams, the adjutant-general at the Battle of Eutaw Springs, was born in Maryland in 1749. Orphaned at a young age, he worked in Frederick, Maryland. Like other Continental officers who served with Major General Nathanael Greene in the south, he had joined the army in 1775 as the War for Independence was inevitable. He joined General George Washington at Boston and served in the northern theater of operations.

When Fort Washington fell to the British, Williams was severely wounded and taken prisoner. First paroled in New York, the parole was revoked as he was believed to have been passing information to General Washington, in violation of parole.

Imprisoned for over a year under the harshest conditions, Williams survived when many of the American prisoners did not. Exchanged for British officers taken by the Americans,

Williams took command of the Maryland Regiment having been promoted to colonel during his time in prison.

Colonel Williams accompanied General Gates in the campaign in the south which ended, for Gates, at the Battle of Camden. Gates appointed him deputy adjutant-general. When Major General Nathanael Greene took command of the Southern Army, Williams was promoted to adjutant-general and he retained this position as long as he served with Greene. After the Battle of Eutaw Springs in which he again distinguished himself as a superior officer, he was promoted to Brigadier General in May, 1782.

After the war, Otho Williams returned to Maryland and settled in Baltimore, Maryland, where he was Collector of Ports. He died in 1800.

Lt. Col. John Eager Howard was born in Maryland in 1752 into a wealthy family and was educated in the manner of the affluent at that time. Like other officers at Eutaw Springs, he had joined the Continental Army at the beginning of the Revolutionary War. Like others he had served in the northern theater of operations and had moved to the south with General Gates. He fought at the Battle of Camden and withdrew into North Carolina with the defeated army.

When Major General Nathanael Greene took command of the Southern Army he assigned Howard to Brigadier General Daniel Morgan's Flying Army which moved to the western area of the territory. At the Battle of Cowpens, where Morgan defeated the British under Lt. Col. Banastre Tarleton, Lt. Col. Howard commanded the infantry.

Howard accompanied Morgan and Greene in the 'race to the Dan,' fought bravely at Guilford Courthouse, Hobkirk's Hill, and Ninety-Six. At Eutaw Springs he made a final bayonet charge and was seriously wounded in the shoulder.

After the war, Howard returned to Maryland and served that state as governor, then as a senator. He served in the

War of 1812 and then ran, unsuccessfully, for the vice-presidency. He died in 1827 and is buried in Baltimore. There is a monument to John Eager Howard in a square in the city of Baltimore.

Lt. Col. Henry Lee was born on 29 January 1756 to a powerful and wealthy Virginia family. He was educated at Princeton and was considered to possess "a fine genius." He intended to study law in England. When the hostility between England and the colonies became apparent, his plans changed. Like the other Continental officers at Eutaw Springs he had joined the army shortly after the Battle of Lexington as a captain of cavalry. He served in the northern theater and was recognized as a fearless and dependable leader. He was most often referred to as Light Horse Harry as he commanded light cavalry troops who had proved to be especially effective in mobile combat operations.

When Major General Nathanael Greene first moved to take command of the Southern Army, Lee did not accompany him but joined Greene later at Hicks Creek in December 1780. Greene dispatched Lee down the PeeDee River to join forces with patriot militia Brigadier General Francis Marion.

After the Battle of Cowpens, Greene recalled Lee to join his army in 'the race to the Dan.' Lee's Legion of horse and foot served actively in North Carolina prior to and during the Battle of Guilford Courthouse. As General Greene turned his attention to South Carolina Lee was once again posted with Francis Marion's militia. The combined force of Lee and Marion forced the surrender of the British at Fort Watson and Fort Motte. His service in the push to move the British out of South Carolina and Georgia is covered in this manuscript.

After the war Lee returned to Virginia where he served as governor. Still active in the military affairs of the country he was promoted to the rank of brigadier general. However, family responsibilities and financial difficulties plagued him and he spent a year in prison for his debts. While there he wrote ***The Revolutionary War Memoirs of General Henry Lee,*** a very interesting account which has been widely quoted in this work. Lee's work has been accused of self-aggrandizement, and it is certain that humility was not one of his virtues. However, his candor caused considerable controversy, especially his criticisms of Thomas Jefferson. Later pro-Jefferson historians attempted to discredit Lee but his work is exceptionally literary even if, in writing it several years after the war, some of the details are in error. The work demonstrates that Lee very likely possessed a certain genius especially in his facile use of the language. In fact, it is Henry Lee who is credited with the remark at the death of George Washington: "First in war, first in peace, first in the hearts of his countrymen."

A firm believer in a central government with a strong national army (this view is know as Federalism) Lee did not avoid serious controversy. He was involved in a riot in Baltimore in which some of his companions were killed and he was severely beaten and seriously injured. When he did not regain his health he left the country to recuperate in Nassau. The change of climate did not improve his health, and realizing that he had little time left, he sailed for home.

Feeling that his death was near, Lee asked to be put ashore at Dungeness, the plantation home of Major General Nathanael Greene, at Cumberland Island on the coast of Georgia. Although the general and his wife were deceased, the Greene family welcomed Lee. Knowing of the great friendship which had existed between General Greene and Lt. Col. Lee, Greene's daughter, Louisa Shaw, and her husband, cared for Lee until his death. It is reported that when Revolutionary veterans realized that Light Horse Harry was in the area they flocked to visit with the charismatic cavalryman whom they greatly respected.

Henry Lee died 25 March 1818 at the Greene home and was buried at Dungeness. Later his remains were removed from Georgia and now repose in the Lee family crypt at the Lee Chapel and Museum on the campus of Washington and Lee University in Lexington, Virginia.

General Robert Edward Lee, Commander of the Army of Northern Virginia during the War Between the States, was the son of Henry Lee and his second wife, Ann Carter.

Lt. Col. William Washington was born 28 February 1752 in Virginia on his father's plantation. Prior to the Revolutionary War William was preparing to enter the ministry but, with the onset of hostilities, he joined the patriot cause shortly after the Battles of Lexington and Concord. He served in the northern theater as an infantry officer in which capacity he served exceptionally well under fire. When the General of the Army, George Washington, was able to mount cavalry, William was assigned to the Continental cavalry. There is no suggestion of nepotism (William and George were second cousins, once removed) as William was a superb horseman and had already demonstrated coolness under fire, and an ability to command. He had already been wounded at least once and possibly more.

William Washington served in the northern theater, then moved to the south and became familiar with the terrain before the Fall of Charleston. The tremendous loss of Continental troops at Charleston did not include Washington's cavalry, and he campaigned in the back country against the British cavalry officer, Lt. Col. Banastre Tarleton. When Nathanael Greene took command of the Southern Army, he was well aware of William Washington's abilities having fought along side him at Trenton. Assigned to Brigadier General Daniel Morgan's Flying Army, Washington commanded the cavalry at Hammond's Store, and then at Cowpens.

Washington's Continental Cavalry accompanied Greene's Army in the 'race to the Dan', then fought at Guilford Courthouse. Moving back into South Carolina Washington's Virginia Continentals were engaged in all the action.

Washington had been wounded in other engagements but his most serious wound was one he received at Eutaw Springs. Pinned under his wounded and dying horse, Washington was taken prisoner and evacuated with the British when they retreated to Charleston. Washington reported to Greene that he had been wounded in the breast with a bayonet and suffered a contusion when he fell as his horse was killed.

The Americans held many British officers of equal rank to Washington for whom he might have been exchanged, but the British refused to exchange him. The fact that he was related to General George Washington was undoubtedly the reason. However, William was trusted to go between Greene's camp and the British camp when the British wished to communicate.

Although a prisoner, William had the opportunity to court Jane Elliot, one of the wealthiest young women in the colony. They were married in Charleston on 21 April 1782, while the British still held the city.

After the British withdrew from Charleston and the war was over, William remained in South Carolina and became a planter on Jane's family estates.

William was a member of the South Carolina General Assembly and was offered an opportunity to run for governor. He declined citing the reason that he had not been born in the state. Also, he did not like to speak and, evidentally, did not care to write as there is little evidence that he ever wrote of his Revolutionary War experiences. Much of his attention was focused on breeding and racing horses.

The South Carolina Washingtons kept in touch with cousin George Washington. When President George Washington made his trip to the south, he declined invitations to stay in private homes. The only exception was his stay in the home of William and Jane.

William died on 6 March 1810 at the age of fifty eight. He is buried in the Elliot cemetery in Ravenel, near Rantowles Bridge, in South Carolina.

Captain Robert Kirkwood. Born in Delaware in 1756 he attended what is now the University of Delaware. Six months before the American Revolution, Kirkwood was commissioned an officer in the Delaware Regiment. Active in the conflict from the first battle at Long Island until the end of Nathanael Greene's reoccupation of South Carolina and Georgia, Kirkwood distinguished himself as a superior officer.

After the disastrous Battle at Camden where 50% of the Delaware troops were killed or captured, the remainder of the regiment was brigaded with the Maryland Regiment. Kirkwood commanded the Delaware troops. With Greene's Southern Army, Kirkwood would fight at Cowpens, Guilford Court house, Hobkirk's Hill, Ninety-Six and at Eutaw Springs.

After the war, with money given to him by Delaware in recognition of his service, he purchased land in the North West Territory (the part of Ohio which had not been the Western Reserve of Connecticut). Later Virginia gave Kirkwood additional acres in Belmont County in what is now southern Ohio along the Ohio River. The Americans had gained this territory from England as part of the Revolutionary War settlement. It had been Indian country and the Indians were incited by the British to resist the new settlers.

Kirkwood was involved in building forts to protect the new territory. In November 1791, at Fort Recovery (near

Dayton, Ohio) Kirkwood was killed and scalped when the Indians attacked. He was one of 700 casualties. Although the battle in which he was killed was his 33rd fight, he was only 35 years old. There is a memorial to Robert Kirkwood at Fort Recovery.

Lt. Col. Richard Campbell. Although Campbell did not survive the Battle of Eutaw Springs, his military career should be noted here. Born in Virginia, Campbell was commissioned in 1776 and fought Indians in the Ohio territory in 1778. Relieving Fort Laurens in 1779, he commanded that post. Promoted to lieutenant colonel, he and his Virginians joined Major General Nathanael Greene in North Carolina just before the battle of Guilford Courthouse. He continued to serve with Greene's army at Hobkirk's Hill, the Siege at Ninety-Six, and at Eutaw Springs.

The account of his death at Eutaw Springs is very interesting. Lt. Col. Henry Lee writes:

> Of six commandants of regiments bearing Continental commissions, Williams and Lee were only unhurt. Washington, Howard and Henderson were wounded; Lieutenant-Colonel Campbell, highly respected and beloved, was killed. The excellent officer received a ball in his breast, in the decisive charge which broke the British line, while listening to an interrogatory from Lieutenant-Colonel Lee, then on the left of the Legion infantry, adjoining the right of the Virginians, the post of Campbell. He dropped on the pummel of his saddle speechless, and was borne to the rear by Lee's orderly dragoon, in whose care he expired, the moment he was taken from his horse. (Lee, 1812:473).

A footnote declares that the report Dr. Ramsey made concerning Campbell's death was in error. That account indicates that Campbell lived long enough to hear that the enemy was in full retreat, to which he remarked: "I die contented."

Johnson (1822), who took every effort to discredit Lt. Col. Lee, uses this discrepancy to indicate that Lee fabricated the event. That does not necessarily follow. Lee left Campbell with an orderly and continued the battle. He believed Campbell died on the ball's impact. In a battle which was as ferocious as this, confusion reigned. With hours of black powder weapons and cannon discharging, little of the field would have been visible. It is possible that Campbell was knocked unconscious by the impact yet rallied long enough to learn the outcome of the battle.

There is a precedent in that very battle. The inert body of Militia General Andrew Pickens was removed from the field and believed dead from a wound to the upper body. The bullet had hit the buckle on his sword belt and had driven it into his breast bone. He had lost consciousness from the impact. The wound was severe but he survived.

Whether Lt. Col. Campbell died instantly as Lee relates, or lived to issue the dramatic words related by Dr. Ramsey, is lost to history. Nevertheless, he died in battle, courageously commanding his troops. The dead were buried on the field and, since no records exist to suggest those dead were ever removed, he rests beside Lake Marion in South Carolina, far removed from his Virginia home.

PATRIOT FORCES- MILITIA

Militia Brigadier General Andrew Pickens. Andrew Pickens was born in Pennsylvania in 1739. His family was part of the Scots-Irish migration which had arrived from Ulster and landed in ports along the north east coast. Finding land too expensive for their meager means, many moved south along the Great Wagon Road. The Pickens family eventually moved to the Waxhaws and then settled in western South Carolina where land was cheap or free to Protestant settlers. Andrew established a post at Long Cane (now Abbeville, South Carolina) to trade with the Indians. Early he fought Indians when the settlements were attacked.

After the fall of Charleston, Pickens took a parole but renounced it in late 1780 as he charged that the British had violated the terms agreed upon. About the same time, Major General Nathanael Greene took command of the Continental Army in the South. When Brigadier General Daniel Morgan needed militia support it was Andrew Pickens to whom he turned. Pickens called on the back country militia to muster at Cowpens. Pickens, a devout Presbyterian, was reputed to rarely speak and never smile. However, he was widely known and respected in the back country for his protection of the settlers against Indian, British and Tory foes. Militia units, all independent commands, responded to his call and over one thousand militia (mostly riflemen) arrived at Cowpens where they were instrumental in Morgan's victory over Tarleton.

Pickens supported Greene's strategy from Cowpens to Eutaw Springs where he was severely wounded. However, he recovered sufficiently to campaign against the Cherokee in October 1782, a year after the battle of Eutaw Springs.

After the war Pickens served in the South Carolina legislature and in Congress. He built a plantation at Tomassee in western South Carolina where he and his wife raised a large family. Andrew Pickens died in August 1817 and is buried at the Old Stone Church Cemetery in the Pendleton District.

Militia Brigadier General Francis Marion. Francis Marion, the Swamp Fox, was born in the winter of 1732 in coastal South Carolina, into a family of French Huguenots. He was twenty-five when he first saw military service, toward the end of the French and Indian War, when the Cherokees threatened western South Carolina. In an attack against Indians in ambush near the town of Echoe, Marion cleared the way for the advancing army. There is a plaque at the Mineral Museum of North Carolina at Spruce Pine commemorating this event.

With the action over Marion returned to the life of a planter and moved in the 1770's to a plantation on the Santee River called Pond Bluff. It was here he heard of the Lexington and Concord events and went immediately to Charleston and joined the Second Regiment as a captain. His first major engagement was at the successful defense of Sullivan's Island, later named Fort Moultrie, on 28 June 1776, where Marion commanded the artillery.

Continuing to serve in the coastal area of South Carolina Marion was, by the time of the British siege of Charleston in 1780, a lieutenant colonel commanding the Second South Carolina Regiment of the Continental Line. Injured before the surrender of Charleston, he had been removed from the city and was hidden in the area along the Santee River while the British troops moved from Charleston to Camden. When he was able to ride, he reported to the Continental Army in North Carolina. Major General Gates was not impressed with Marion and his entourage of men and boys, black and white, poorly armed but well mounted. He was sent to gather intelligence. One of the black men who rode with Marion throughout the war was his own slave, Oscar, whom he called 'Buddy.'

When the Williamsburg militia asked for Marion to command them, Gates concurred and Marion missed disastrous action at the Battle of Camden. This militia became the nucleus of what became known as Marion's Brigade and fought many actions in the next two and a half years. Marion's guerilla operations embarrassed the British and intimidated the Loyalists as he moved through the floodplains of the Wateree, Black, Santee and PeeDee Rivers. He held no territory and established no permanent headquarters. He stayed in safe houses when possible but always maintained access to escape routes.

Both William Dobein James and Lt. Col. Henry Lee rode with Marion and their descriptions of him suggest a small, unattractive, wiry man who was withdrawn and moody. He had a basic education but was not considered highly literate. His knowledge was based on experience and Lee rates that highly. Marion's grasp of tactics was extraordinary as evidenced by his survival when the British sought to destroy him. Lee suggests he was brave but not reckless, and he was always reluctant to risk the lives of his men needlessly. This practice of inflicting the maximum damage with the minimum number of casualties may, in part, explain why his followers were so loyal.

Francis Marion became the militia leader that Greene depended upon during the late stages of the Southern Campaign. He served at Greene's command until shortly before the British evacuation of Charleston when he dismissed his men and returned to the ruins of Pond Bluff. In his fifties, he married his cousin, Mary Esther Videau. With her money he was able to rebuild his plantation. Rankin reports that Marion, his wife and his slave, Oscar, would travel around the sites of his campaign and visit old friends from the militia days.

Although Marion was returned time and again to the South Carolina legislature, he was not a skilled politician. His main political interest was in public education and he advocated free schools. It would be many generations before this was accomplished.

Francis Marion died on 27 February 1785 at sixty-three. He was buried in the cemetery of his brother's plantation,

Belle Isle, which adjoined Pond Bluff. The site is on the Santee River near St. Stephen, South Carolina.

The commanders at the Battle of Eutaw Springs were not the only heroes. The men who engaged in that battle of close to four hours, known as the bloodiest battle of the American Revolution, must have been extraordinary. To have fought in the heat, on little rest, half-rations and a limited supply of water suggest a determination which deserves respect.

Although the actual casualty figures are difficult to ascertain, Participants who reported wading through puddles of blood on the field were probably not exaggerating.

The dead were buried on the field. There is no record of them ever being moved. They are still there, making this ground a cemetery as well as a battle site.

ENDNOTES

1. Considerable research has been done on the Battle of Camden in particular and on the Southern Campaign in general. The website, Documentary History of the Battle of Camden, contains extensive primary source material.

    http://battleofcamden.org

2. In addition to the biographies of Nathanael Greene by Francis Vinton Greene and Elswyth Thane, there is an excellent account of Greene's background in "A General from Rhode Island" in *The Road to Guilford Courthouse* by John Buchanan. Also, there is a wealth of Greene's correspondence on the internet and published in other references.

3. In searching for Lt. Col. Alexander Stewart it is important to note that his name is spelled various ways by scholars. Although some historians spell the name **Stewart,** others use **Stuart.** A third spelling is found in Roderick McKenzie's Strictures, "**Col. Steuart**." Similarly, the rank is sometimes designated as Lieutenant Colonel, others as Colonel, and occasionally General as it appears he held that rank later. The Alexander Stewart who served at Eutaw Springs was an officer of the 3rd Regiment of Foot and was born circa 1740 and died in December 1794.

4. Most of the provincial units who served in South Carolina were raised in the North: The New Jersey Volunteers, New York Volunteers, DeLancey's Brigade, the Volunteers of Ireland, the British Legion, etc. One unit in which many South Carolinians fought was the South Carolina Royalists who were organized in Florida of men who had fled South Carolina. If one wishes to learn more about these Americans who remained loyal to the King, there is much material on the Internet. In searching, remember that although Americans refer to these people as Tories, the correct name is **United Empire Loyalists**. Occasionally, the term **British Empire Loyalist** is used.

There are many Canadian sites which chronicle the lives of these Loyalists who settled in Canada after the war. One site which contains much material about the units which were provincial, and thus 'Loyalist', is the Loyalist Institute site. The material there is extensive and well maintained.

http://www.royalprovincial.com

5. For South Carolina Loyalists, see Lambert, listed in References. Loyalist militia commanders in South Carolina include Col. William (Bloody Bill) Cunningham, David Fanning, Thomas Brown, John Waters, and others. To read further on these leaders, see Lambert.

6. A British officer who distinguished himself at the Battle of Eutaw Springs is **Major John Marjoribanks** (pronounced Marshbanks). He died as the result of his wounds and is buried at the battle site. His name is often spelled **Majoribanks**. The British spelling and the family spelling appear on the grave at the Eutaw Springs battle site.

It reads:

**John Marjoribanks
Inf.late major of the 19th Regt.
And commanding a flank battn
of His Majesty's Army died 22 of Oct. 1781**

7. Williams' report gives only surnames. The Christian names are taken from Rankin's text. Rankin asserts that "The North Carolina Brigade suffered greater losses than any other Continental unit; 154 casualties." (Rankin 1971:360).

8. *There is a discrepancy between this report and the list in the National Archives and Records Administration. The latter lists those with asterisks as wounded. Colonel Williams' report does not list any wounded cavalry but we must assume from the account of Washington's charge that there were wounded officers.

9. **These men belonged to Marion's Brigade. James writes: "General Marion had many of his men and Col. Hugh Horry wounded; but fewer killed than at Quimby; among the latter was the brave Capt. John Simons, of Pedee." (James 1821: 137)

10. Col. James Hayes was the commander of the patriot Little River Militia (Greenville, SC area) and had been a hero of both King's Mountain and the Battle at Cowpens.

11. Tradition has it that Cunningham, in his haste, left everything and his sword was claimed as a trophy by Butler and handed down through that family. The sword was gifted by the Butler family to the McKissick Museum of the University of South Carolina and is presently in their collection.

12. The incident of 30 August referred to was Marion's attack on Major Fraser's South Carolina Royalists on the causeway at Parker's Ferry. That date is approximate.

BIBLIOGRAPHY

Babits, Lawrence E. (1998). *A Devil of a Whipping: The Battle of Cowpens.* Chapel Hill, NC: The University of North Carolina Press.

Baker, Thomas E. (1998). *Another Such Victory.* Eastern National.

Barefoot, Daniel W. (1999). *Touring South Carolina's Revolutionary War Sites.* Winston Salem, NC: John E. Blair Publisher.

Bass, Robert (1974*). Swamp Fox: The life and campaigns of General Francis Marion.* Orangeburg, SC: Sandlapper Publishing Co., Inc.

Borick, Carl P. (2003). *A Gallant Defense: The Siege of Charleston, 1780.* Columbia, SC: The University of South Carolina Press..

Buchanan, John. (1997). *The Road to Guilford Courthouse.* New York: John Wiley and Sons, Inc.

Carrington, Henry B. (1876). *Battles of the American Revolution 1775-1781 Historical and Military Criticism with Topical Illustrations.* New York: A. S. Barnes & Company.

Cook, Don (1995). *The Long Fuse: How England Lost the American Colonies, 1760-1785.* New York: The Atlantic Monthly Press.

Edgar, Walter. (1998). *South Carolina: A History*. Columbia, SC: The University of South Carolina Press.

Edgar, Walter. (2001). *Partisans and Redcoats: The Southern Conflict That Turned the Tide of the American Revolution.* New York: William Morrow & Company, Inc.

Fortesque, J. W. (1911) *History of the British Army. Vol. 3.* London: McMillan and Sons.

Frierson, John L. Transcriber. *Francis Marion's Order Book 1781-1782.*

Gibbes, R. W. (1853). *Documentary History of the American Revolution consisting of Letters and Papers Relating to the Contest for Liberty, Chiefly in South Carolina in 1781 and 1782.* Columbia, SC: Banner Steam-Power Press. (Reproduced in 1972 by the Reprint Company, Post Office Box 5401, Spartanburg, SC 29301).

Greene, Francis Winton. (1893). *General Greene.* New York: Appleton and Company. (Reprinted by Heritage Books Inc., Bowie, Maryland in 2002.)

Haller, Stephen E. (2001). *William Washington: Cavalryman of the Revolution.* Bowie, Maryland: Heritage Books, Inc.

James, William Dobein. (1821*). A Sketch of the Life of Brig. Gen. Francis Marion and A History of His Brigade From His Rise in June 1780 until Disbanded in*

December, 1782 (With Descriptions of Characters and Scenes not Heretofore Published). Published in Charleston, SC. (Reprinted in 1948 by Continental Book Company, Marietta, Georgia).

Johnson, William. (1822). *Sketches of the Life and Correspondence of Nathanael Greene, Major General of the Armies of the United States in the War of the Revolution(Compiled chiefly from original materials).* Charleston, SC: A. E. Miller.

Katcher, Philip R. N. (1973). *Encyclopedia of British, Provincial and German Army Units 1775-1783.* Harrisburg, PA: Stackpole Company.

Lambert, Robert S. (1987). *South Carolina Loyalists in the American Revolution.* Columbia, SC: The University of South Carolina Press.

Lee, General Henry. (1812). *The Revolutionary War Memoirs of General Henry Lee.* Edited by Robert E. Lee Republished by Da Capo Press, New York, 1998.

Lumpkin, Henry. (1981). *From Savannah to Yorktown: The American Revolution in the South.* New York: Paragon House Publishers.

Morrell, Dan L. (1992). *Southern Campaign of the American Revolution.* Baltimore, Maryland: The Nautical and Aviation Publishing Company of America.

Murray, Stuart. (1998*).* *The Honor of Command: General Burgoyne's Saratoga Campaign, June-October 1777.* Bennington, Vermont: Images from the Past.

O'Kelley, Patrick (2004). *Nothing but Blood and Slaughter:The Revolutionary War in the Carolinas, Vol.*

Two 1780. Booklocker.com.Inc.

O'Kelley, Patrick.(2005). ***Nothing but Blood and Slaughter: The Revolutionary War in the Carolinas. Vol. Three, 1781.*** Booklocker.com.Inc.

Pancake, John S. (1985). ***This Destructive War: The British Campaign in the Carolinas, 1780-1782.*** Tuscaloosa, Alabama:The University of Alabama Press.

Rankin, Hugh F. (1973). ***Francis Marion: The Swamp Fox.*** New York: Thomas Y. Crowell Company.

Rankin, Hugh F. (1976). ***Greene and Cornwallis: The Campaign in the Carolinas.*** Raleigh, NC: Office of Archives and History . North Carolina Department of Cultural Resources.

Rankin, Hugh F. (1971). ***The North Carolina Continentals.*** Chapel Hill, NC: The University of North Carolina Press.

Reiss, Oscar. (1998). ***Medicine and the American Revolution.*** Jefferson, NC: McFarlane & Company, Inc.

Schenck, David. (1889*).* ***North Carolina 1780-1781:Being a History of the Invasion of the Carolinas by the British Army under Lord Cornwallis in 1780-81.*** Raleigh, NC: Edwards & Broughton, Publishers. (Reprinted by Heritage Books Inc., Bowie, Maryland in 2000)

Stokesbury, James L. (1991). ***A Short History of the American Revolutionary.*** New York: William Morrow and Company, Inc.

Wright, Robert K., Jr. (1989). ***The Continental Army.*** Washington, D.C.: Center of Military History, United States Army.

INDEX

ALLEN, Lt Col Isaac 97
ARMSTRONG, Maj 82 107
ASHE, Col 82 107
AUGUSTA, GA 12 60 67
BENNINGTON, 3
BLACK MINGO, Battle 87
BLACKSTOCK'S FARM, Battle 33 86
BLOUNT, Maj 82 107
BLUE SAVANNAH, Battle 87
BRATTONSVILLE 86
BREED'S HILL 3
BRITISH ARMY, 1
  Regulars:
  3rd Regiment of Foot, 94
  19th Regiment of Foot, 96
  30th Regiment of Foot, 96
  63rd Regiment of Foot, 94
  64th Regiment of Foot, 55 94
  71st Regiment of Foot (Fraser's Highlanders), 18 20 45
  84th Regiment of Foot, 94
  Provincials:
  DeLancy's New York Brigade, 97
  New Jersey Volunteers, 20
  New York Volunteers, 20
  South Carolina Regiment Of Royalists, 98 99
BROWNE, Capt 85
BURGOYNE, Gen John 3 29 30
CAMDEN, 12 16 21 Battle 18 33 49 55
British Evacuation 57
CAMPBELL. Col Richard x 82 Eutaw Springs 101-113 Death 115 Notes 154-155
CANTEY'S PLANTATION 123
CAREY'S FORT, Battle 16
CARLTON, Sir Guy 129
CASUALTIES, American Officers 116-117
CATAWBA RIVER, 12
CEDAR SPRINGS, Battle 16
CHARLESTON, 1 10 33 53 Evacuation 131
CHARLOTTE, NC 18 28 29
CHATHAM, Lord (William Pitt) 3
CHERAW, 12
CLARKE, Col Elijah 27 At Blackstock's 33 To Augusta 60 Smallpox 89 War Against the Cherokees 131
CLEVELAND, Col 27
CLINTON, Sir Henry 10 12 14 At New York 128 Force at New York 128
COATES, Col Quimby Bridge 96
COFFIN, Maj John At Hobkirk's Hill 57 Eutaw Springs 99 136
CONCORD, 2
CONTINENTAL ARMY, 3 25 29 36 79 Loss at Charleston 10

INDEX

CONTINENTAL ARMY (cont)
  Artillery 85 Casualties 116
  Delaware 18 65 82
  Lee's Legion 82
    Casualties 116
  Maryland 18 65 82
    Casualties 116
  North Carolina 82
    Casualties 116
  Virginia 82 Casualties 116
  Virginia Cavalry 83
    Casualties 116
CORNWALLIS, Lord Charles 10 12 14 16 18 21 27 28 33 36 Race to the Dan 41- 44 At Guilford Battle 44-47 Decision 47-48 At Wilmington 50
COWPENS, 20 Battle 36-41 82 88
CRUGER, Col At Ninety-Six 61 Eutaw Springs 97 106
CUNNINGHAM, Col William 129-130
DAN RIVER, Race 41-44
DOHLA, Johann Conrad Diary Entry 142
DYSENTERY, (Camp Fever) 68
EDMUNDS (EDMONDS), Capt Thomas 82
EUTAW SPRINGS, x 1 Battle 101-113
FERGUSON, Patrick 16
  At King's Mountain 20-

FERGUSON (cont) 24 27 33 67
FERGUSON'S SWAMP, 120
FINN, Capt 85
FISHING CREEK, 86
FORT MOTTE, 53 57 Battle 58 87
FORT MOULTRIE, 10
FORT WATSON, 53 55 87
FORT WILLIAMS, 33
FRAZER, Maj of SC Royalists Captures Col Isaac Hayne 63
  At Parker's Ferry 71
FREEMAN'S FARM, 3
GAINES, Capt William 85
GATES, Gen Horatio 16 25 28
GEORGETOWN, 12
  British Evacuate 60 87
GERMAIN, Lord 6 8 12 14 128
GOWEN'S OLD FORT, Battle 16
GREENE, Col Joseph 97
GREENE, Gen Nathanael x 1 25 Background 25-27 Moves south 27 Strategy 28 Divides Army 29 Race to the Dan 41-44 At Guilford 44-47 New Strategy 51-53 Battle of Hobkirk's Hill 55-57 Meets Marion 58 At Ninety-Six 60-62 At the High Hills 65

INDEX

GREENE (cont)
  Move Toward Eutaw Springs 74-76 Battle Of Eutaw Springs 101-113 Ferguson's Swamp 120 Return to High Hills 123 Leaves High Hills 128 Route to Eutaw Springs 73-76 Battle of Eutaw Springs Official Report 137 Report to General Washington 137 Report to Congress 138 Report to Varnum 138 After the War 145-146

GUILFORD COURTHOUSE,
  Battle 44-47 49 50 81 82

HALFWAY SWAMP,
  Battle 87

HAMMOND'S STORE, 33

HAMPTON, Wade xi 85
  Commanded Picket 118 136

HANGING ROCK, 12
  Battle I 16 Battle II 16 86

HARDMAN, Maj Henry 81

HAYNE, Col Isaac
  Captured 63 Hanged 70

HENDERSON, Col William 85

HEAT STROKE, 68

HICK'S CREEK, 31 50

HIGH HILLS OF THE SANTEE, 64-66

HOBKIRK'S HILL,
  Battle 55-57 81 82

HOWARD, John Eager x 28 Flying Army 31 At Cowpens 36-41 80 81 Eutaw Springs 101-113 Notes 148-149

HOWELL'S FERRY 76

KING GEORGE III, 2 3 6 8 10 12 14 128

KING'S MOUNTAIN,
  Battle 20-24 49 67 86

KIRKWOOD, Robert xi 28 Flying Army 31 At Cowpens 36-41 Eutaw Springs 101-113 Notes 153-154

LACEY, Col 27

LEE, Henry x Joins Marion 31-32 Re-Joins Marion 53 At Fort Watson 55 To Fort Granby 60 To Augusta 60 At Quimby Bridge 69 Legion 83 Eutaw Springs 101-113 Notes 149-151

LEXINGTON, 2 3

LOWER BRIDGE OF THE BLACK RIVER Battle 87

LOYALIST (Tory), 6 12 20 58

MAHAM, Maj At Fort Watson 55

MALMEDY, Marquis de Col At Eutaw Springs 88 106

INDEX

MARJORIBANKS, Maj John 96 Eutaw Springs 106-113 136
MARION, Francis x 18 27 28 Joined by Lee 31 50 Rejoined by Lee 53 At Fort Watson 55 Meets Greene 58 To Georgetown 60 At Quimby Bridge 69 Parker's Ferry 71-75 Eutaw Springs 101-113 Ferguson Swamp 118 At Peyre's 76 101 123 142 123 Senator 130 Notes 156-159
McARTHUR, Maj 102 120
McCALL, Maj James At Hammond's Store 33 Dies of Smallpox 88
McDOWELL, Col 27
McKAY, Lt 55
McPHERSON, Lt 58
MILITIA AT EUTAW, South Carolina 86 Marion's Brigade 87 North Carolina 88
MONCK'S CORNER, 14 119
MORGAN, Gen Daniel 6 27 28 Background 29-30 Flying Army 30-31 Battle Of Cowpens 36-41 Illness Forces from Action 44 50
MOUNT HOPE SWAMP. Battle 87
MUSGROVE'S MILL, Battle 16 20 86

MYERS, Thomas Pension Application 124
NELSON'S FERRY, Flooded 73-74 76 Battle 87 102
NINETY-SIX, 12 20 21 33 Battle 60-63 81 82
NORTH, Lord 3 6 128 Resigns 129
OVERMOUNTAIN MEN, 20 27 King's Mt 20-24
PARKER'S FERRY 71-75 76
PATRIOT MILITIA, At Cowpens 36-41
PEE DEE RIVER, 12 18
PEYRE'S PLANTATION, 76 101 122 123
PICKENS, Andrew x 27 At Cowpens 36-41 50 53 To Augusta 60 Eutaw Springs 101-113 Representative 130 War Against the Cherokees 131 Notes 155-156
PITT, William (Lord Chatham) 3
PNEUMONIA, 68
QUIMBY BRIDGE, (Quinby Bridge) Battle 69 87
RACE TO THE DAN, 41-44
RAMSOUR'S MILL, Battle 16
RAWDON, Lord 18 33 53 At Battle of Hobkirk's

INDEX

RAWDON (cont) Hill 55-57 Control Shrinks 60 To Ninety-Six 61-62 Relinquishes Command To Col Stewart 63 Concurs Hanging Hayne 63 Smallpox 66
RIVER ROAD, 101
ROCHE HOUSE, Eutaw Springs 101
ROCKY MOUNT, 12 Battle 16 86
ROOTING PARTY 103
RUTLEDGE, Gov Thomas Reestablishes State Government 130 Letter to Marion 141
SAMPIT BRIDGE, Battle 87
SANTEE RIVER, 1 18
SARATOGA, 16 29
SAVANNAH, 1
SEVIER, Col 28 50 Ordered To Join Greene 70
SHELBY, Col Isaac 20 27 51 Ordered to Join Greene 70
SHERIDAN. Maj 98 112
SINGLETON'S MILL, Battle 87
SMALLPOX, 66-67
SNEAD (SNEED), Maj 82 107
SOUTH CAROLINA STATE TROOPS, 86 Casualties 117
STEWART, Col Alexander Takes Command 63 To Thomson's 64 To

STEWART (cont) Eutaw Springs 76 At Eutaw Springs 101-113 Report to Lord Cornwallis 118-119 At Ferguson's Swamp 120
SULLIVAN'S ISLAND, 10 87
SUMNER, Gen Jethro x 82 Eutaw Springs 101-113 Notes 146-147
SUMTER, Gen Thomas 27 To Orangeburg 60 At Blackstock's 33 50 53 Dog Days 69 Battle at Quimby Bridge 69 Not at Eutaw Springs 85-86 Senator 130
TARLETON, Banastre 14 16 28 33 At Cowpens 36-41 Race to the Dan 41-44 Yellow Fever 67 82
TEARCOAT SWAMP, Battle 87
THOMSON'S PLANTATION, 64 69 76
TYPHOID FEVER, 68
TYPHUS, 67-68
TRENTON, 3
UTI POSSIDETIS, 51
WASHINGTON, Gen George 2 3 6 12 25 26 27 Inoculation Policy 66
WASHINGTON, William x 27 28 Flying Army 30 At Hammond's Store 33 At Cowpens 36-41 Guilford 49 Cavalry 84 Eutaw Springs 101-113

WASHINGTON (cont)
  Notes 151-153
WATEREE RIVER, 12 18
WATSON, Col John 53 95
WAXHAWS, 14
WILLIAMS, Otho x 28 80
  Battle of Eutaw Springs
  101-113 Report on
  Eutaw Springs 139
  Notes 147-148
WILLIAMSBURG
  MILITIA, 18
WILLIAMSON'S
  PLANTATION,
  Battle 16
WILMINGTON, 47 49 50
WINNSBORO, 21 29 33
WYBOO SWAMP, Battle
  87
YELLOW FEVER, 67-
  68
YORKTOWN, 1 33 53
  Naval Battle 126 Siege
  126 Surrender 126

ABOUT THE AUTHORS

CHRISTINE SWAGER

Christine Swager was born in St. Stephen, New Brunswick, Canada, the descendent of a United Empire Loyalist (Tory) who left New York after the British lost the Revolutionary War. She learned her history from British textbooks. Swager came to the United States as a college student and earned a B.A., cum laude, from Kent State University, an M.A. from the University of Denver, and a Ph. D. from The University of South Carolina. After moving around the country with her military husband, they settled in South Carolina.

While teaching at USC she was approached by teachers and urged to write for them and their students about the Revolutionary War. The first two books, ***Black Crows and White Cockades,*** and ***If Ever Your Country Needs You***, chronicle the campaigns of Francis Marion, "the Swamp Fox." The third, ***Come to the Cow Pens***! is the story of that historic battle.

Swager and her husband live in Santee, South Carolina, just a few miles from the site of the Battle of Eutaw Springs. Since there is renewed interest in preserving Revolutionary War battle sites, ***The Valiant Died*** puts this battle in perspective, not only in regard to Lord Cornwallis and his Southern Campaign, but also focuses on Major General Nathanael Greene's Southern Campaign.

JOHN ROBERTSON

In his own words, John Robertson is a "map nut." Retired from business and living in western North Carolina, he was befriended by historian Dr. Bobby Moss, who became his mentor. The two tramped through many long-forgotten battle and skirmish sites and John became intrigued with the importance of terrain on where and how battles were fought.

This led him to eighteenth century mapping.

The needs of Dr. Moss and Dr. Swager focused the work on maps of the locations of the Southern Campaign. He also supplies maps for articles in *Southern Campaigns of the American Revolution.*

Robertson is the editor of http://battleofcamden.org which he describes as "arguably the most thoroughly documented website for any battle," and a must for those interested in the American Revolution. Other web sites which reflect his many interests are: http://jrshelby.com and http://jrshelby.com/sc-links.htm

Robertson is an interpreter for the National Park Service at Cowpens National Battlefield. His next major project will be to create a cd atlas/gazetteer for the locations in Patrick O'Kelley's four volume work, **Nothing but Blood and Slaughter.** Indeed, Robertson is an ambitious map nut.

John Robertson and his wife reside in Shelby, North Carolina.

CPSIA information can be obtained at www.ICGtesting.com
Printed in the USA
LVOW122233230513

335345LV00009B/108/P